P9-DZX-954

2nd Edition

THE DIFFERENTIATED CLASSROOM

2nd Edition

THE DIFFERENTIATED CLASSROOM

Responding to the Needs of All Learners

Carol Ann Tomlinson

ASCD | Alexandria, VA USA

1703 N. Beauregard St. • Alexandria, VA 22311-1714 USA
Phone: 800-933-2723 or 703-578-9600 • Fax: 703-575-5400
Website: www.ascd.org • E-mail: member@ascd.org
Author guidelines: www.ascd.org/write

Gene R. Carter, *Executive Director*; Richard Papale, *Acting Chief Program Development Officer*; Stefani Roth, *Interim Publisher*; Genny Ostertag, *Acquisitions Editor*; Julie Houtz, *Director, Book Editing & Production*; Katie Martin, *Editor*; Lindsey Smith, *Graphic Designer*; Mike Kalyan, *Manager, Production Services*; Keith Demmons, *Production Designer*; Andrea Wilson, *Production Specialist*

Copyright © 2014 ASCD. All rights reserved. It is illegal to reproduce copies of this work in print or electronic format (including reproductions displayed on a secure intranet or stored in a retrieval system or other electronic storage device from which copies can be made or displayed) without the prior written permission of the publisher. By purchasing only authorized electronic or print editions and not participating in or encouraging piracy of copyrighted materials, you support the rights of authors and publishers. Readers who wish to reproduce or republish excerpts of this work in print or electronic format may do so for a small fee by contacting the Copyright Clearance Center (CCC), 222 Rosewood Dr., Danvers, MA 01923, USA (phone: 978-750-8400; fax: 978-646-8600; web: www.copyright.com). To inquire about site licensing options or any other reuse, contact ASCD Permissions at www.ascd.org/permissions, or permissions@ascd.org, or 703-575-5749. For a list of vendors authorized to license ASCD e-books to institutions, see www.ascd.org/epubs. Send translation inquiries to translations@ascd.org.

All referenced trademarks are the property of their respective owners.

All web links in this book are correct as of the publication date below but may have become inactive or otherwise modified since that time. If you notice a deactivated or changed link, please e-mail books@ascd.org with the words "Link Update" in the subject line. In your message, please specify the web link, the book title, and the page number on which the link appears.

PAPERBACK ISBN: 978-1-4166-1860-7   ASCD product #108029

ASCD Member Book No. FY14-7 (May 2014, P). ASCD Member Books mail to Premium (P), Select (S), and Institutional Plus (I+) members on this schedule: Jan, PSI+; Feb, P; Apr, PSI+; May, P; Jul, PSI+; Aug, P; Sep, PSI+; Nov, PSI+; Dec, P. For up-to-date details on membership, see www.ascd.org/membership.

Also available as an e-book (see Books in Print for the ISBNs).

Quantity discounts: 10–49 copies, 10%; 50+ copies, 15%; for 1,000 or more copies, call 800-933-2723, ext. 5773, or 703-575-5634. For desk copies: www.ascd.org/deskcopy.

Library of Congress Cataloging-in-Publication Data

Tomlinson, Carol A.
  The differentiated classroom : responding to the needs of all learners / Carol Ann Tomlinson. -- Second edition.
    pages cm
  Includes bibliographical references and index.
  ISBN 978-1-4166-1860-7 (pbk. : alk. paper) 1. Individualized instruction. 2. Cognitive styles in children. 3. Mixed ability grouping in education. I. Title.
  LB1031.T65 2014
  371.39'4--dc23
                                      2014000806

23 22 21 20 19 18 17   4 5 6 7 8 9 10 11 12

THE DIFFERENTIATED CLASSROOM

Responding to the Needs of All Learners

Preface to the Second Edition

She waited until they were all in their usual places, and then she asked, "Did I choose you, or did you choose me?" And the Souls answered, "Yes!"

E. L. Konigsburg, *The View from Saturday*

This book has now been a two-part journey for me. I wrote the first edition, published in 1999, shortly after leaving my public school classroom and the 20-plus-year teaching career that grounded me as an educator and as a human being. Those years were still fresh in my thinking and breathing and were full of nostalgia then. I told my new colleagues at the University of Virginia that I would always be a middle school teacher first, if for no other reason than that I would not have as long a career at the university as I had had in public school. My powers of prognostication were a bit off—as they often are. As I conclude the revision that will be the second edition of *The Differentiated Classroom*, I have been at the university longer than I was in the public school classroom.

Many things have changed over the past 15 years. Classrooms that once had few if any English language learners in their student mix now teach students from many parts of the globe. Whereas in 1999, there was precious little classroom technology available for teachers and students, now technology routinely opens classrooms to the world and to a world of ways to think about teaching and learning. Today, we know much more about the science of teaching and learning than we did then, and educators in the United States and many other countries have been through multiple national conversations focused on what and how we teach our children. And, of course, more educators are familiar with differentiated instruction. Some even consider differentiated instruction a fundamental expectation for teachers in today's classrooms.

Nonetheless, many things have remained the same for me and in schools and classrooms. At heart, I am still a middle school teacher who is grateful for the opportunity to know and learn from the research side of my profession. And in schools, classroom practice still tilts decidedly to the one-size-fits-all end of the flexibility spectrum. Arguably, a relentless focus on raising test scores has resulted in curriculum and instruction that are, if anything, less dynamic than they were 15 years ago. There is still an untenable gap in the school experiences of students from low-income backgrounds and students of color compared to the school experiences of white students and students from more economically secure backgrounds.

Both the similarities and differences in me and in the world of education made writing the second edition of *The Differentiated Classroom* intriguing and compelling. There was more thinking to be done, more to learn, more opportunity to get it right.

While writing the first edition, I was struck by the realization that teaching is always, in part, a writing of history. I reflected on my own history as a teacher and felt connected to the teachers who came before me, especially those who worked in one-room schoolhouses. These teachers accepted all comers and said by their actions, "I'm grateful for every one of you who is here to learn. Different as you are, we can make this work." I was also transported back to late nights at the home of my first real teaching partner, and how she and I worked to make sense of multitask classrooms, which seemed to be what our very diverse students very obviously needed. I recalled the names and faces of students I taught and who unfailingly taught me more. They were high schoolers, preschoolers, and middle schoolers. They were so alike, yet so different. They needed me to be many things to them, and they taught me how to do that. I was also reminded of colleagues in Fauquier County, Virginia, who worked hard, took professional risks, thought "outside the box," found joy in classrooms, and created joy there too. It was a classy school district, even though at the time it was rural, small, and not on the radar of many people beyond its boundaries. It was also a great training ground for teaching because there was encouragement to be innovative in service of kids.

Writing the second edition of the book has involved retracing my steps on the journey of my "second life" at the University of Virginia and in schools across the United States and well beyond its borders. I am now privileged to work with teachers throughout the world and with all the varieties of students who are its future. My colleagues at the university push my thinking and model excellence. My students remain my best teachers. They ask, "Why?" and inevitably follow with, "Why not?"

In places near and far, other teachers' questions create patterned tapestries of common understanding and shared uncertainty, which are generally seedbeds for growth. Having the opportunity to write a second edition has been a catalyst for reflecting on how my thinking has changed. It's comforting when a passage penned 15 years ago still sounds sensible to me. It's also reassuring to realize that my thinking is sharper now, which allows me to tighten and refocus parts of the original book. And it's humbling to realize that despite a steady conversation over 15 years about teaching that responds to the needs of learners, we still gravitate to the familiar and convenient and comfortable patterns that dominated our work a decade and a half—and a half-century—ago.

Teachers now, as they did in 1999, still typically ask the same questions about teaching and differentiation. "How do you grade it?" "How can we differentiate instruction if our goal is a standardized test?" "Won't my students be angry if they don't all have the same piece of work?" "How can a classroom be fair if all students don't get the same _____ (homework, version of a test, time to complete work, etc.)?"

We've grown as teachers in the last decade and a half. We are more focused and more amenable to accountability—although perhaps not focused on better things and likely held accountable for questionable measures of success. We are less naïve. Some of us are more tech-savvy. In many schools, we have more informed and more sustained dialogue about substantive aspects of our work.

And yet, we still tend to teach our students as though they were essentially alike. We still measure and label and sort them as though we've lost sight of their essential humanity. We still have pockets of brilliant pedagogy and caverns of indefensible pedagogy just miles or blocks or hallways apart. We still serve some of our students well and many poorly. We still "cover" curriculum that is handed to us more often than we generate informed invitations for students to explore the disciplines and the world.

I suppose my students—past and present—have made me an optimist. I choose to see both the evidence of positive change in our profession and the evidence of resistance to change as opportunities to continue thinking, to continue looking for words and images that can contribute to a more humane and productive way to be a teacher. The principles in this second edition of *The Differentiated Classroom* are as compelling to me as they were the first time I put them on paper and the first time I tested them under the tutelage of my middle school students.

Another question that is as common now as it was in 1999 is, "How can I find time to differentiate instruction? It's hard, and I'm so busy already!" Time and experience have reinforced the only answer I know to give: "Build a career. Plan to be better tomorrow than today, but don't ever plan to be finished or to be 'good enough.'" As I once heard a teacher say to a student in her classroom, "Of course it's hard. That's why it's worth your time. And you can do hard things."

Teaching is about learning, learning is about becoming, and making a history is about taking up a profession and making a life. This book is about writing your own history as a teacher—one day at a time, one increment of growth at a time, one collegial partnership at a time. I hope you find it helpful in that quest.

Before we begin, I would like to express my gratitude to all those teachers who have shaped my life for the better. Some of them are called colleagues, some students, some editors, some authors, some friends—but they are all teachers, and I am so much stronger for their presence in my world.

Finally my profound respect goes out to the teachers everywhere who resolutely refuse to teach at the same level of proficiency and professionalism they reached today and continue to look ever forward and ever upward. You are the life-shapers among us.

C.A.T.

1

What Is a Differentiated Classroom?

So many students are physically present and psychologically absent. About 40 percent of students go through the motions, neither trying hard nor paying attention. So many cut class and are truant, so many admit to cheating to get through, so many lose interest because they cannot keep up, and so many are bored by the lack of appropriate challenge. So many do not learn that ability is not enough and effort is crucial. About half of students who drop out say their classes were not interesting, and about two-thirds say not one teacher cared about their success in learning at school. Not all is rosy with teachers, teaching, and school.

Adapted slightly from John Hattie, *Visible Learning*

More than a century ago in the United States and other parts of the world, the teacher in a one-room schoolhouse faced a challenging task. She had to divide her time and energy between teaching young people of varied ages who had never held a book and could not read or write along and teaching more advanced students of varying ages who had very different content needs. Today's teachers still contend with the essential challenge of the teacher in the one-room schoolhouse: how to reach out effectively to students who span the spectrum of learning readiness, personal interests, and culturally shaped ways of seeing and speaking about and experiencing the world.

Although today's teachers generally work with individual classes where students are approximately the same age, these children arguably have an array of needs greater than those of the children in the one-room schoolhouse. Thus, a teacher's question remains much the same as it was 100 years ago: "How do I divide time, resources, and myself so that I am an effective catalyst for maximizing talent in all my students?"

Consider how these teachers answer that question.

• Ms. Handley studies her students persistently; she feels she must know them well to teach them well. She sets as her measure of professional success that every student engages in and contributes to learning every day and that every student makes observable progress every day. She works hard to gain her students' trust very early in the year and to prove herself worthy of their trust thereafter. She uses formative assessment, both formal and informal, as her primary understanding of what each student needs in order to connect with the curriculum and to grow as a result of class experiences. She says that formative assessment lets her know what she needs to do to make tomorrow's lesson work best for every student.

• Mrs. Wiggins assigns students to multiple spelling lists based on pre-assessment results rather than making the assumption that all 3rd graders should work on List 3.

• Mr. Owen matches homework to student need whenever possible, trying to ensure that practice is meaningful for everyone. He invites students to be part of determining which home tasks will best help them understand and apply mathematical concepts and principles.

• Ms. Jernigan sometimes teaches math to the whole class at once. More often, she uses a series of direct instruction, practice, and application groups based on daily formative assessment information. She matches practice activities and sense-making tasks to students' varied readiness needs, and she groups students for real-world math applications based on their interests or preferred approaches to learning. In this way, she says, students learn from and contribute to the learning of a variety of peers.

• Ms. Enrico offers students two or three options when it's time for them to develop a final product or complete an authentic assessment at the conclusion of a unit. She bases the options on students' interests so they have the chance to link what they've learned with something that seems important and relevant to them as individuals. She also often offers a "Let's Make a Deal" option through which students can propose their own product formats, making certain that the learning outcomes that students need to demonstrate remain constant across options. Students use Wikispaces Classroom to develop their projects, which allows Ms. Enrico to monitor their progress throughout the process.

• Mr. Raules encourages English language learners to do initial drafts of writing in their first language if that helps them express their ideas. He also ensures that, as often as possible, students have access to some online or print resource materials in their first languages so they can more readily understand and relate to important concepts.

• Ms. Willoughby "flips" her classroom at key instructional points when it makes sense for students to explore new content at home and practice their newly developing skills and ideas in class. She carefully monitors students' understanding with "entry cards" or other types of formative assessment and creates instructional groups when it makes sense for students to work together toward common learning goals. She moves among the groups or sits with them to coach and mentor student progress.

• Mr. Ellis works regularly with small-group instruction he designs to move students forward from their current points of knowledge, understanding, and skill. Students with whom he's not meeting at a given time work independently, in pairs or in small groups, on practice or sense-making tasks set at appropriate challenge levels or tailored to connect current content to students' interests. Formative assessment guides his instructional planning.

All of these teachers are differentiating instruction. They may have practiced differentiation before it had a name. They are simply teachers who strive to do whatever it takes to ensure that struggling, advanced, and in-between learners; students with varied cultural heritages; and children with a broad array of background experiences all grow as much as they possibly can each day, each week, and throughout the year.

Hallmarks of Differentiated Classrooms

In differentiated classrooms, teachers begin with two critical "givens": there are content requirements—often in the form of "standards"—that will serve as destination points for their students, and there are students who will inevitably vary as learners. Thus, teachers in differentiated classrooms accept and act on the premise that they must be ready to engage students in instruction through different approaches to learning, by appealing to a range of interests, and by using varied rates of instruction along with varied degrees of complexity and differing support systems. In differentiated classrooms, teachers ensure that students compete against themselves as they grow and develop more than they compete against one another, always moving toward—and often beyond—designated content goals.

In other words, teachers who differentiate provide specific alternatives for individuals to learn as deeply as possible and as quickly as possible, without assuming one student's road map for learning is identical to anyone else's. These teachers believe that students should be held to high standards. They work diligently to ensure that all students work harder than they meant to; achieve more than they thought they could; and come to believe that learning involves risk, error, and personal triumph. These teachers also work to ensure that all students consistently experience the reality that success stems from hard and informed work.

Teachers in differentiated classes use time flexibly, call upon a range of instructional strategies, and become partners with their students so that both what is learned and the learning environment are shaped to support the learner and learning. They do not force-fit learners into a standard mold; these teachers are students of their students. They are diagnosticians, prescribing the best possible instruction based on both their content knowledge and their emerging understanding of students' progress in mastering critical content. These teachers are also artists who use the tools of their craft to address students' needs. They do not aspire to standardized, mass-produced lessons because they recognize that students are individuals and require a personal fit. Their goal is student learning and satisfaction in learning, not curriculum coverage.

Teachers in differentiated classrooms begin with a clear and solid sense of what constitutes powerful curriculum and engaging instruction. Then they ask what it will take to modify that curriculum and instruction so that each learner comes away with knowledge, understanding, and skills necessary to take on the next important phase of learning. Essentially, teachers in differentiated classrooms accept, embrace, and plan for the fact that learners bring to school both many commonalities and the essential differences that make them individuals.

Differentiated classrooms embody common sense. The logical flow of thought in a differentiated classroom is this: a nurturing environment encourages learning. Quality curriculum requires clear and compelling learning goals used in ways that engage students' minds and lead to understanding. Persistent formative assessment guides both teacher and students toward essential goals. Instruction works best when it's carefully aligned with content goals and fashioned to address the needs indicated by both formal and informal formative assessment. Classroom management must allow for both predictability and flexibility in order for a range of students to achieve essential goals. Although this sequence of logic is more or less common sense, nonetheless it can be difficult to achieve—as common sense often is. In part, it can be difficult to implement and plan for effectively differentiated classrooms because we see few examples of good ones. There *are* such examples, however, and they offer a productive way to start exploring differentiated instruction.

Portraits from Schools

Teachers work daily to find ways to reach out to individual learners at their varied points of readiness, interest, and preferred approaches to learning. There is no single "right way" to create an effectively differentiated classroom; teachers craft responsive learning places in ways that match their own personality and approach to teaching. Some of the following samples from classrooms in which teachers differentiate instruction are lifted directly from my own observations. Some are composites of several classrooms or extensions of conversations with teachers. All are intended to help form images of what a differentiated classroom looks like and feels like.

Think carefully about the contrasts between examples in which teachers teach with little regard to student variance and those in which teachers plan with student variance in mind. Think about particular students you teach. Which scenario is likely to be a better fit for those students? Why?

Snapshots from Two Primary Classrooms

For a part of each day in Mrs. Jasper's 1st grade class, students rotate among learning centers. Mrs. Jasper has worked hard for several years to provide a variety of learning centers related to several subject areas. All students go to all learning centers because Mrs. Jasper says they feel it's unfair if they don't all do the same thing. Students enjoy the movement and the independence the learning centers provide.

Many times, Isabel breezes through the center work. Just as frequently, Jamie is confused about how to do the work. Mrs. Jasper tries to help Jamie as often as she can, but she doesn't worry so much about Isabel because her skills are well beyond those expected of a 1st grader, and Isabel completes all of the work quite readily and accurately. Today, all students in Mrs. Jasper's class will work in a learning center on compound words. From a list of 10 compound words, they will select and illustrate 5. Later, Mrs. Jasper will ask for volunteers to show their illustrations. She will do this until the students share illustrations for all 10 words.

Down the hall, Ms. Cunningham also uses learning centers in her 1st grade classroom. She, too, has invested considerable time in developing interesting centers on a variety of subjects. Ms. Cunningham's centers, however, draw upon some of the principles of differentiated classrooms. Sometimes all students work in a particular learning center, if it introduces an idea or skill new to everyone. More often, Ms. Cunningham assigns students to a specific learning center or to a particular task at a certain learning center, based on her continually developing sense of their individual readiness.

Today, her students will also do learning center work focused on compound words. Students' names are listed at the center, and beside each name is a sticker in one of four colors. Each student works on a task contained in the folder that matches the color of his or her sticker. For example, Sam has a red sticker next to his name. Using the materials in the red folder, Sam must decide the correct order of pairs of words to make familiar compound words. He also will make a poster that illustrates each simple word and the new compound word they form. Using materials in the blue folder, Jenna will look around the classroom and in books to find examples of compound words. She will write them out and illustrate them in a booklet. Using materials in the purple folder, Tjuana will write a poem or a story that uses compound words she generates and that make the story or poem interesting. She then can illustrate the compound words to make the story or poem interesting to look at as well as to read. In the green folder, Dillon will find a story the teacher has written. It contains correct and incorrect compound words. Dillon will be a word detective, looking for "villains" and "good guys" among the compound words. He will create a chart to list the good guys (correct compound words) and the villains (incorrect compound words) in the story, ultimately correcting the "villains" in the story.

Tomorrow, during circle time, all students may share what they did with their compound words. As students listen, they are encouraged to say the thing they think is best about each presenter's work, based on a checklist of learning goals posted for the assignment. Ms. Cunningham may also spotlight a few students who are sometimes reticent to speak in front of the group, noting something she appreciated about their work and asking them a question that should elicit at least a brief response.

Examples from Two Elementary Classrooms

In 5th grade, students at Sullins Elementary work with the concept of "famous people" to make connections between social studies and language arts. All students are expected to hone and apply research skills, write with a logical flow of ideas, and share with an audience what they understand about the famous people they are studying.

Mr. Elliott asks all his students to select and read a biography of a famous person from the literature or history they have studied. Students then use books from the school library and Internet resources to find out more about the person they have chosen. Each student writes a report about a famous person, describing the person's culture, childhood, education, challenges, and contributions to the world. Students are encouraged to use both original and "found" illustrations in their reports. Mr. Elliott gives the whole class a coaching rubric focused on use of research resources, organization, and quality of language.

In her 5th grade class, Mrs. May gives her students interest inventories to help her identify areas in which they may have a special talent or fascination, such as sports, art, medicine, the outdoors, writing, or helping others. Ultimately, each student selects an area of special interest or curiosity to be his or her focus in an upcoming unit on characteristics of famous people.

Mrs. May's class discusses the fact that in all areas of human endeavor, famous people from many cultures have shaped our understanding and practice in all sorts of fields. Mrs. May reads aloud biographical sketches of a statesman, a musician, an astronaut, a community organizer, a scientist, and an artist. The people she spotlights are both male and female and represent multiple ethnic or cultural groups. Together, students and teacher describe traits and principles related to these famous people.

For example, famous people often are creative, they take risks to make advances in their fields, they tend to be rejected before they are admired, they sometimes fail and sometimes succeed, and they are persistent. Students test these principles as they discuss historic figures, authors, and people in the news today. In the end, students conclude that people can be famous "for the right reasons" or "for the wrong reasons." They decide to research people who became famous by having a positive impact on the world.

The school media specialist helps each student to generate lists of "productive" famous people in that student's particular categories of interest. She also helps them learn how to locate a variety of resources that can help them research famous individuals from varied cultures and time periods (including brainstorming possible interview sources). She talks with them about the importance of selecting research materials they can read and understand clearly, and she offers to help them look for alternatives for materials that seem too easy or too hard for them.

Mrs. May and her students talk about how to take notes and try various ways to take notes during their research. They also consider different methods of organizing their information, such as webs, outlines, storyboards, and matrices, and discuss the approaches that seem to work well for different students in the class. They talk about all the ways they can express what they learn: through essays, historical fiction, monologues, or character sketches. Mrs. May provides students with a rubric that guides them on the content, research, planning, and traits of effective narrative writing. Students also work with Mrs. May individually to set their own personal goals for understandings, working processes, and final products.

As the assignment continues, Mrs. May works with individuals and small groups to assess their understanding and progress and to provide personal coaching. Students also assess each other's work according to the rubrics and individual goals. They ensure that each report shows someone who has made a positive contribution to the world. In the end, the whole class completes a mural in the hallway outside their room that includes the principles related to fame in the shape of puzzle pieces. On each puzzle piece, students write or illustrate examples of the principle from their famous person's life. They then add ways in which they believe the principles are or will be important in their own lives.

Comparisons from the Middle Grades

In Ms. Cornell's science class, students work in a specific cycle: read the textbook chapter, answer questions at the end of the chapter, discuss what they have read, complete a lab, and take a quiz. Students do the labs and complete their reports in groups of four. Sometimes Ms. Cornell assigns students to a lab group as a way of minimizing behavior problems; often, students select their own lab groups. They read the text and answer the questions individually. Ms. Cornell typically conducts two or three whole-class discussions during a chapter. The class works with unit reviews before each chapter test. Students enter the science fair in the spring, with a project based on a topic studied in the fall or winter.

Mrs. Santos often assigns students in her science class to "reading squads" when they work with text or online materials; students of similar reading levels usually work together. Mrs. Santos varies graphic organizers and learning-log prompts according to the amount of structure and concreteness the various groups need to grasp essential ideas from the book chapter, and she provides Internet resources at varied levels of sophistication based on student reading proficiency. Varied reading routines allow students to read aloud with peers or to read silently. The students complete graphic organizers together and respond to writing prompts or blog entries individually. As students work, Mrs. Santos moves among groups or meets with individual students. Sometimes she reads key passages to students or asks them to read to her. She always probes for deeper understanding and helps students to clarify their thinking.

Sometimes Mrs. Santos asks students to complete labs, watch videos, explore models or diagrams online, or work with supplementary materials before they read the chapter so they have a clear sense of the unit's guiding principles to support their later work with text that is complex and abstract. Sometimes they read the text for a while, do a lab or view a demonstration, and go back to the text. Sometimes labs and supplementary materials follow text exploration. She may vary the order of interaction with materials for small groups of students based on their interests or facility with abstract ideas. Frequently, she has two versions of a lab going simultaneously: one that includes scaffolding for students who need concrete experiences to understand essential principles, and one for students who already grasp the important principles and can deal with them in complex and uncertain contexts.

Multiple times in the course of a unit, Mrs. Santos uses formative assessment that aligns tightly with the unit's essential learning outcomes. Thus, she is always aware of which students need additional instruction with key knowledge, understandings, and skills; which students need more advanced applications early in the unit; and who may be having difficulty transferring ideas or skills to new contexts. Students typically have a choice of formats for key performance assessments, with required learning outcomes constant across formats. When students complete summative science projects, a single rubric provides criteria for success that apply across options:

- Work alone or with peers to investigate and address a problem in the community that relates to the topic you are studying.
- Work in a mentorship role with a person or group in the community using the current topic to address a local problem.
- Study scientists past and present who have positively influenced the practice of science in the topic you have studied.
- Write a science fiction story based on the topic you have studied, using accurate science in the context of fiction writing.
- Use classroom cameras to create a narrated photo essay that would help a younger student understand how some facet of the topic you have studied works in the world.
- Propose another option and work with Mrs. Santos to shape a project that demonstrates understanding and skill in science.

In Mrs. O'Reilly's 8th grade English class, students read the same novels and have whole-class discussions on them. Students complete journal entries on their readings. Typically, Mrs. O'Reilly assigns a portion of the novel to read for homework each night, accompanied by a summarization activity or set of follow-up questions to answer.

In Mr. Wilkerson's 8th grade English class, students often read novels that have a common theme, such as courage or conflict resolution. Students select from a group of four or five novels, and Mr. Wilkerson provides classroom sets of the books. He also makes sure the novels span a considerable reading range, tap into several interests, and reflect an array of cultures.

Mr. Wilkerson's students meet frequently in literature circles, where they discuss their ideas with others who are reading the same novel. Although the various literature circles reflect different degrees of reading proficiency, students in each group take turns serving in one of five leadership roles: discussion director, graphic illustrator, historical investigator, literary luminary, and vocabulary enricher. There are printed guides for each role to help students fulfill their responsibilities. Mr. Wilkerson also varies journal prompts and blog entries; sometimes he assigns different prompts or entries to different students, and sometimes he encourages students to select a prompt that interests them. There also are many opportunities for whole-class discussion on the theme that all the novels share, allowing all students to contribute to an understanding of how the theme "plays out" in the book they are reading and in life.

Samples from High School

In Spanish I, Mrs. Horton's students nearly always complete the same language pattern drills, work on the same oral exercises, read the same translation and culture-related passages, and take the same quizzes. They often work individually on their in-class assignments but sometimes practice in pairs or work with small groups to complete a task.

In French I, Mr. Adams's students often work with written exercises at differing levels of complexity and with different amounts of teacher support. Their oral exercises focus on the same basic structures but require different levels of sophistication with the language. Sometimes students can "opt out" of review sessions to create their own French dialogue, read a French-language magazine, or correspond with a French-speaking e-pal. Students often work in teacher-assigned, mixed-readiness pairs to prepare for what Mr. Adams calls "fundamentals quizzes." Students who wish to do so can, from time to time, select a partner to prepare for a "challenge quiz." Success on a challenge quiz nets students homework passes they can use to be excused from homework assignments when their work on the quiz indicates they have mastered the material. Mr. Adams's students self-assess their performance on formative tasks and set personal goals for increased language fluency and proficiency; they also select homework assignments that will best help them achieve those goals. In addition, each student "adopts" a country or region of a country in which French is spoken. During the year, students explore various cultural, social, linguistic, and geographical concepts in "their" country, and they work in groups to compare and contrast French influences across contexts.

In Mr. Matheson's Algebra II class, students typically complete the same homework, check the homework assignments as a whole class, work independently on the same in-class drills, and take the same tests.

In her Algebra II class, Mrs. Wang helps students identify key concepts, principles or big ideas, and skills in a given chapter. After various formative and summative assessments, students are encouraged to look at their own assessment results and select homework assignments and in-class mini-workshops that will help them clarify areas of confusion.

Toward the end of a chapter, Mrs. Wang gives students different "challenge problems," which they can tackle alone or with a classmate. Each student's problem is designed to be a mental reach; Mrs. Wang encourages students to discuss multiple ways of solving the problem and to articulate their thinking as they work through the problem. On end-of-chapter tests, students find challenge problems similar but not identical to the ones Mrs. Wang gave them earlier. There may be 5 or 6 different challenge problems distributed among her approximately 30 students.

In physical education, Mrs. Bowen's students usually all work with the same exercises and basketball drills. Mr. Wharton, on the other hand, helps his students diagnose their starting points with various exercises and basketball skills, set challenging goals for personal improvement, and chart their personal progress. He particularly stresses growth in two areas: those where a student is best and weakest.

In U.S. History, Ms. Roberson and her students cover the information in the text sequentially. She lectures to supplement information in the text and often uses primary documents available on the Internet to have students compare perspectives on events. Ms. Roberson includes a special emphasis on women's history and African American history during months designated by the school for those emphases.

Mrs. Washington's U.S. History students look for key concepts and principles or "big ideas" that recur in each period of history they study, as well as for concepts and big ideas unique to each period. They study different points of view and the experiences shared by various cultural, economic, and gender groups. They use a variety of text, video, audio, and online resources at varying degrees of difficulty and in different languages (to support students who are learning English).

When Mrs. Washington lectures, she always uses PowerPoint slides or whiteboard elements that emphasize key vocabulary and ideas in order to help visual learners. She also pauses throughout the lecture to encourage students to talk with one another and the class about key ideas and to ensure their grasp of those ideas.

Essays and projects often ask students to take their understanding of a period in U.S. history and contrast it with what was going on in another culture or in another geographical area during the same period. Project assignments always offer several options for how students can express their knowledge, understandings, and skills. At the end of each quarter, students can take an exam as their final summative assessment, or they can use an authentic assessment they have modified (with Mrs. Washington's guidance and approval) as half of their final summative grade. Both options require students to demonstrate the knowledge, understanding, and skill designated as essential for the unit.

• • •

Differentiated classrooms support students who learn in different ways and at different rates and who bring to school different talents and interests. More significantly, such classrooms work better for a wide range of students than do one-size-fits-all settings. Teachers in differentiated classrooms are more in touch with their students and approach teaching more as an art than as a mechanical exercise.

Developing classrooms that actively attend to both student similarities and student differences is anything but simple. The chapters that follow describe classrooms with differentiated and responsive instruction, and they offer guidance on how you can, over time, make such a setting a reality for your class or school.

2

The Underpinnings of Differentiation

There is no formula or recipe that works for all learners in all times. There is no set of lesson plans or units that can engage the range of learning styles, approaches, and intelligences that are likely to gather in one classroom.

William Ayres, *To Teach: The Journey of a Teacher*

Most effective teachers modify some of their instruction for students some of the time. Many of those teachers also would say they differentiate instruction, and, to some degree, they do. It is not this book's goal, however, to recount the sorts of modifications that sensitive teachers make from time to time, such as offering a student extra help during lunch or asking an especially able learner a challenging question during a class discussion. This book offers guidance for educators who want to regularly develop and facilitate consistent, robust plans in anticipation of and in response to students' learning differences.

The Nature of Differentiated Classrooms

Although there is no single image of what a differentiated classroom should look like, there are some characteristics common in most of the classrooms that are focused on the success of each learner. In important ways, these shared characteristics reveal the nature of differentiation. They give differentiation its definition. Thinking about key characteristics of differentiated classrooms is useful in constructing a sense of the nature and intent of differentiated instruction.

The Learning Environment Actively Supports Learners and Learning

In differentiated classrooms, the learning environment is seen as key to student success. Teachers work as consciously and purposefully in maintaining an inviting learning environment as they do in designing curriculum or implementing instruction. In fact, they see the three elements—environment, curriculum, and instruction—as firmly linked. They also understand that learning environment has an impact on students' affective needs and that affect, in turn, plays a role in cognition and learning. Toward this end, teachers in differentiated classrooms help students understand that

- They are welcomed and valued as they are.
- The teacher is confident of their capacity to learn what they need to learn and will support them vigorously as they do so.
- They will work together to enhance one another's growth.
- Both successes and failures are inevitable in the learning process, and this classroom is a safe place for both.
- Hard work will result in observable growth.
- Routines and processes in the classroom are designed to give all students access to whatever they need for success.

The Teacher Actively Attends to Student Differences

From a very young age, children understand that some of us are good at kicking a ball, some at telling funny stories, some at manipulating numbers, and some at making people feel happy. They understand that some of us struggle with reading words from a page, others with keeping tempers in check, and still others with arms or legs that are weak. Children seem to accept a world in which we are not alike. They do not strive for sameness but rather search for the sense of personal triumph that comes when they are respected, valued, nurtured, and even cajoled into accomplishing things they believed beyond their grasp.

Teachers in differentiated classrooms are well aware that human beings share the same basic needs for nourishment, shelter, safety, belonging, achievement, contribution, and fulfillment. They also know that human beings find those things in different fields of endeavor, according to different timetables and with different support systems. These teachers understand that by attending to human differences they can best help individual students address common needs. Our experiences, culture, gender, genetic codes, and neurological wiring all affect how and what we learn. There is no illusion that a single lesson plan will work effectively for every learner, no intent to offer a "take it or leave it" approach to learning. Rather, teachers who practice differentiation accept as a given that they will need to create a variety of paths toward essential learning goals and to help students identify the paths that work best in achieving success.

These teachers understand that some students need additional instruction to enable more confident understanding of last year's math, while others will find this year's math insufficiently challenging. They know that some students who are learning English will do so as a matter of course, while others must struggle mightily. They realize that every student brings talents to the classroom that must be recognized, tapped, and developed, and they also grasp that these won't be the same talents or even the talents traditionally championed in school. Practitioners of differentiation also realize that some students need frequent reassurance to offset how life at home erodes their self-confidence. They see that some students respond much better to gentle humor than to admonition, and that others see sternness as a display of respect. They recognize that painfully shy students may need to do their "speaking" on paper before they're ready to do so in front of the class, while other students enthusiastically embrace the classroom as a stage. They understand that some students benefit from guidance on how not to alienate their peers and that others need help in taming their humor so it isn't overwhelming. In other words, teachers who seek to reach each learner also seek to respond to the cognitive and affective variance that is inevitable among learners.

The Curriculum Is Organized to Support Learning

No one can learn everything in every textbook, let alone in a content area or discipline. The brain is structured so that even the most able of us will forget more than we remember about most topics. It is crucial, then, for teachers to articulate what's essential for learners to know, understand, and be able to do in a given domain.

In differentiated classrooms, teachers carefully fashion curriculum around the essential knowledge, understanding, and skills of each subject. Students should leave the class with a firm grasp of that knowledge, understanding, and skills, but they won't leave with a sense that they have conquered all there is to know.

Clarity about what matters most in a topic increases the likelihood of introducing it in a way that each student finds meaningful, interesting, and appropriate. Clarity ensures struggling learners don't drown in a pool of disjointed facts and information; it ensures advanced learners spend their time grappling with important complexities rather than repeating work or simply accruing more data. Clarity also ensures that teacher, learners, assessment, curriculum, and instruction are linked tightly in a journey likely to culminate in personal growth and individual success for each child.

Understanding likely learning progressions or instructional sequences in key content areas helps the teacher determine next steps for learners based on their particular entry points and current learning status. To use an analogy, if the goal is for students to travel from Miami to Boston, the teacher keeps an eye on each student's daily journey toward the final destination. He has no intention of having some students only make it to Atlanta or having others end up in Los Angeles. On the other hand, there are many highways and side roads that lead to Boston, as well as varied modes of transportation and timetables available. In no way does the teacher feel compelled to have every student travel exactly the same distance each day or always use the same mode of transportation.

Assessment and Instruction Are Inseparable

In differentiated classrooms, assessment is diagnostic and ongoing. It provides teachers with day-to-day data on students' readiness for particular ideas and skills, their interests, and their approaches to learning. These teachers don't see assessment as something that comes at the end of a unit to find out what students learned (or didn't learn); rather, assessment is today's means of understanding how to modify tomorrow's instruction.

Formative assessment data may come from small-group discussion among the teacher and a few students, whole-class discussion, journal entries, portfolio entries, exit cards, skill inventories, pre-tests, homework assignments, student opinion or interest surveys, teacher observation of students using targeted checklists of competencies, and a host of other mechanisms. Such formal and informal assessment yields an emerging picture of who understands key ideas and who can perform targeted skills, at what levels of proficiency, and with what degree of interest. The teacher then shapes tomorrow's lesson—and even reshapes today's—with the goal of helping individual students move ahead from their current position of competency. Further, the teacher understands that a pivotal classroom goal is to help students take charge of their own learning—to help them seek awareness of learning goals, become increasingly conscious of their status relative to those goals, and make plans that support their movement steadily toward (and perhaps beyond) the goals. Encouraging students to analyze their own work relative to clearly articulated goals and criteria for success helps them consistently grow in independence, agency, and self-efficacy as learners.

At benchmark points in learning—such as the end of a unit segment or of the unit itself—teachers in differentiated classrooms, like most teachers, use summative assessments to formally record student growth. Even then, however, they use varied means of assessment so that all students can fully display their skills and understanding. Assessment always has more to do with helping students demonstrate what they know, understand, and can do than with cataloging their mistakes.

The Teacher Modifies Content, Process, and Products Based on Student Readiness, Interest, and Learning Profile

The teacher in the differentiated classroom thoughtfully uses assessment data to guide modifications to content, process, product, or learning environment. *Content* is what teachers want students to learn from a particular segment of study, or the materials or mechanisms through which students gain access to that important information. *Process* describes activities designed to ensure that students use key skills to make sense of, apply, and transfer essential knowledge and understandings. *Products* are vehicles through which students demonstrate and extend what they have learned.

Students vary in readiness, interest, and learning profile. *Readiness* is a student's entry point relative to particular knowledge, understanding, or skills. Students with less developed readiness may, for example, need

• Someone to help them identify and make up gaps in past learning so they can move ahead;
• More opportunities for direct instruction or practice;
• Activities or products that are more structured or more concrete, with fewer steps, closer to their own experiences, requiring simpler reading skills; or
• A more deliberate pace of learning.

Advanced students, on the other hand, may need

- To skip practice of previously mastered skills and understanding;
- Activities and products that are complex, open-ended, abstract, and multifaceted, drawing on advanced reading materials; or
- A brisk pace of work—or perhaps a slower pace to allow for greater depth of exploration of a topic.

Readiness is not fixed, and so many students will struggle at some point and many will be advanced at one time or another. Readiness is *not* a synonym for ability!

Interest refers to a learner's affinity, curiosity, or passion for a particular topic or skill. One student may be eager to learn about fractions because she is very interested in music and her math teacher has explained how fractions relate to music. Another learner may find a study of the American Revolution fascinating because he is particularly interested in medicine and has been given the option of creating a final product on medicine during that period. Another student may relate to *Romeo and Juliet* only after he learns that it parallels a familiar story from his own primary culture.

Learning profile has to do with the ways in which a learner learns. It may be shaped by intelligence preferences, gender, culture, or learning style. Some students need to discuss concepts with peers to learn them well. Others work better alone and through writing rather than group discussion. Whereas some students learn easily from part-to-whole, others need to see the big picture before specific parts make sense. Some students prefer logical or analytical approaches to learning. Other classmates prefer creative, application-oriented lessons. It's not unusual for a student to benefit from one approach to learning in math, for example, and another in history or English—or from one approach when content is familiar and another when it is new. The goal ought not to be to label or pigeonhole students as particular "kinds" of learners but rather to offer varied ways of approaching learning and then helping students determine which of those ways—or others they may propose—seem most effective in supporting their learning at a given time.

Teachers may adapt one or more of the curricular elements (content, process, products) based on one or more of the student characteristics (readiness, interest, learning profile) at any point in a lesson or unit (see Figure 2.1). However, teachers need not differentiate all elements in all possible ways in every unit. Effectively differentiated classrooms include

Figure 2.1 Differentiation of Instruction

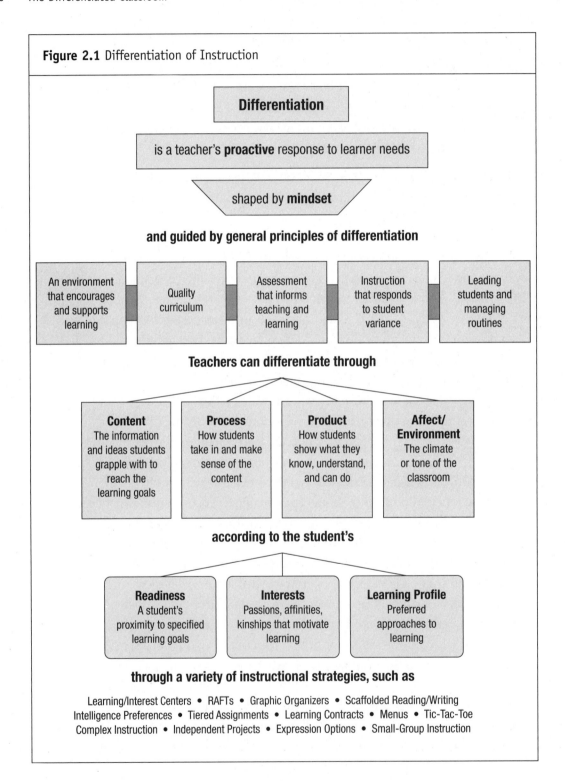

many times in which whole-class, nondifferentiated fare is the order of the day; other times when the teacher differentiates based on students' interests; and still other times when carefully formed, mixed-readiness groups are useful. It makes sense to modify a curricular element only when (1) there is a student need for doing so and (2) you have reason to believe the modification increases the likelihood that learners will understand important ideas and use important skills more thoroughly.

The Teacher and Students Collaborate in Learning

Teachers are the chief architects of learning, but students should assist in essential ways with the design and building. It is the teacher's job to know what constitutes essential learning, to diagnose, to prescribe, to vary the instructional approach based on content goals and student needs, to ensure smooth functioning of the classroom, and to see that time is used wisely. Nonetheless, students have much to contribute to classroom organization, functioning, and effectiveness.

Students can provide diagnostic information, develop classroom rules, participate in the governing process grounded in those rules, learn to use time as a valuable resource, and actively help one another learn. Students can let teachers know when material or tasks are too hard or too easy, when learning is interesting (and when it isn't), when they need help, and when they are ready to work alone. When they are partners in shaping all parts of the classroom experience, students develop ownership of their learning and become more skilled at understanding themselves, appreciating one another, and making choices that enhance their own learning as well as that of their classmates. They become effective partners for their peers and for the teacher.

In a differentiated classroom, the teacher is the leader; like all effective leaders, she attends closely to her followers and involves them thoroughly in the journey. Together, teacher and students plan, set goals, monitor progress, analyze successes and failures, and seek to multiply successes and learn from failures. Some decisions apply to the class as a whole. Others are specific to an individual.

A differentiated classroom is, of necessity, student-centered. Students are the workers. The teacher coordinates time, space, materials, and activities. Her effectiveness increases as students learn to help themselves, their teacher, and one another achieve group and individual goals.

The Teacher Balances Group and Individual Norms

In many classrooms, a student is an "unsuccessful" 5th grader if he falls short of 5th grade "standards." That the student made more progress than anyone in the room counts for little if he still lags behind grade-level expectations. Similarly, a child in 5th grade is generally expected to continue doing 5th grade tasks even though she achieved two years ago the standards or other criteria around which the tasks are developed. About that student, we often say, "She's fine on her own. She's already doing well."

Teachers in a differentiated classroom understand expected norms and attend to them consistently. They also understand individual norms. When a student struggles as a learner, the teacher has two goals. One is to accelerate the student's current knowledge, skills, and understanding as rapidly as is possible for that learner, while ensuring genuine understanding and meaningful application of essential skills. The second is to ensure the student's steady growth toward or beyond group goals. In other words, teachers in differentiated classes work toward learning outcomes designated as critical for students of a particular age or grade level. Those teachers also understand, however, that pathways to the group goals must necessarily be suited to an individual; that the journey will not be lockstep; and that a particular set of goals, although highly desirable for some students, may be limiting for others. Thus a teacher in a differentiated class keeps track of student status relative to group goals as well as to individual growth over time.

A great coach never achieves greatness for himself or his team by working to make all his players alike. To be great, and to make his players great, he must make each player the best that he or she possibly can be at a given time. No weakness in understanding or skill is overlooked, but all players work from their strengths and competencies, not from a sense of deficiency. There is no such thing as "good enough" for any team member. There is always a next step to take. In an effectively differentiated classroom, assessment, instruction, feedback, and grading take into account both group and individual goals and norms, while coaching students to continue to develop their own particular capacities as learners and as human beings.

The Teacher and Students Work Together Flexibly

Just as an orchestra is composed of individuals, varied ensemble groups, sections, and soloists, the differentiated classroom is built around individuals, various small groups, and the class as a whole. They all work to "learn to play the score," albeit with varied instruments, solo parts, and roles in the whole. Sometimes, they practice in sections or individually; other times, they practice together. The goal of all the work is to enhance the musical proficiency of each member of the group while working toward a common and meaningful performance.

To address the various learning needs that make up the class as a whole, teachers and students work together in a variety of ways. They use materials flexibly and employ flexible pacing. Sometimes the entire class works together, but sometimes small groups are more effective. Sometimes everyone uses the same materials, but it is often effective to have a variety of materials available. Sometimes everyone finishes a task at 12:15; often, some students finish a task while others need additional time for completion.

Sometimes the teacher determines who will work together, and sometimes students make the choice. When the teacher decides, she may group students based on similar readiness, interest, or learning profile needs for particular purposes. Other times, for other purposes, she places students of differing readiness, interests, or learning profiles together. Sometimes students' task assignments are random. In other words, grouping is both highly flexible and fluid. Student groupings are responsive to both student needs and content goals, and tasks within groups are designed to draw on the strengths of the individuals in those groups. The teacher does not see students as "bluebirds" or "buzzards," and she ensures that students do not see themselves or one another in those terms, either. Sometimes the teacher is the primary helper of students, and sometimes students are each other's best source of help.

In a differentiated classroom, the teacher also draws on a wide range of instructional strategies that help her focus on individuals and small groups, not just the whole class. Sometimes learning contracts are helpful in targeting instruction; at other times, independent investigations work well. The goal is to link learners with essential understandings and skills at appropriate levels of challenge and interest.

Figure 2.2 contrasts some ways in which approaches to teaching may vary in differentiated versus nondifferentiated classrooms. Feel free to add your own comparisons to the chart as you think about your own classroom and as you read through the rest of the book. Remember that there is much middle ground between an absolutely traditional classroom and an absolutely differentiated one (assuming either extreme could ever exist).

Figure 2.2 Comparing Classrooms

The Traditional Classroom	The Differentiated Classroom
Student differences are often masked or acted upon when problematic.	Student differences are valued and studied as basis for planning.
Assessment is most common at the end of learning to see who "got it."	Assessment is ongoing and diagnostic to understand how to make instruction more responsive to learner needs.
A relatively narrow sense of intelligence prevails.	Focus on a range of intelligences is evident.
The teacher believes some students are smart and some are not smart and teaches accordingly.	The teacher believes all students have the capacity to succeed and supports that belief through "teaching up" and differentiated instructional plans.
A single definition of *excellence* exists.	*Excellence* is defined in terms of both individual growth and recognized norms.
Student interest is infrequently tapped.	Students are frequently guided and supported in making interest-based choices.
Relatively few approaches to learning are offered.	Many approaches to teaching and learning are consistently evident.
Whole-class instruction dominates.	Many instructional groupings are used.
Coverage of texts, curriculum guides, or content goals define the limits of instruction.	Student readiness, interest, and approach to learning guide instructional plans.
The focus of learning is the mastery of facts or the use of skills out of context.	Use of essential knowledge and essential skills to achieve or extend essential understandings is the focus of learning.
Single-option assignments are the norm.	Multi-option assignments are common.
Time is relatively inflexible.	Time is used flexibly and in accordance with student needs.
A single text prevails.	Multiple materials and other resources are provided.
A single interpretation of ideas or events or single right answers are typically sought.	Multiple perspectives on ideas, issues, and events are routinely sought.
The teacher directs student behavior.	The teacher facilitates development of student skills of self-reliance and collaboration.
The teacher solves most classroom problems.	Students help other students and the teacher solve problems.
A single form of assessment is most often used.	Students are assessed in multiple ways and in multiple modes.
The grading process communicates only performance, not process or progress.	The grading process reflects student performance, work processes, and growth.

For an interesting self-assessment, think of the two columns in Figure 2.2 as continuums. Place an X on each continuum where you believe your teaching is now, and place a check mark where you'd like your practice to be.

Three Pillars That Support Effective Differentiation

There is no patented formula for creating a differentiated classroom. Rather, effective differentiation is governed by a philosophy, a set of principles, and some pivotal instructional practices. Said another way, differentiation is *heuristic*, or principle-driven, rather than *algorithmic*, or formula-driven.

Figure 2.3 illustrates the three components that frame and inform robust differentiation. In the remainder of this chapter, we'll examine the first of the three pillars: the philosophy that shapes differentiated classroom practice. The second and third columns—principles and instructional practices key to the success of differentiation—will be explored in Chapters 4 through 8.

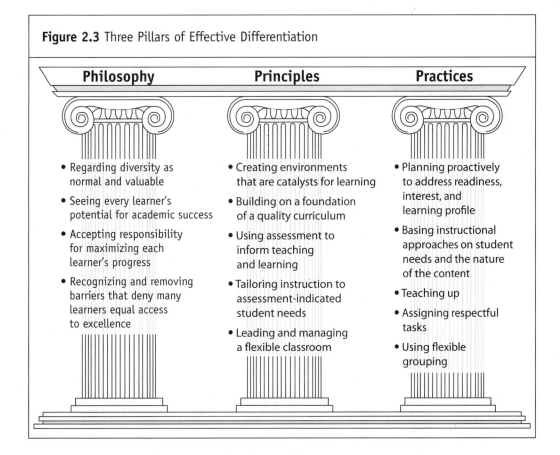

Figure 2.3 Three Pillars of Effective Differentiation

Philosophy	Principles	Practices
• Regarding diversity as normal and valuable	• Creating environments that are catalysts for learning	• Planning proactively to address readiness, interest, and learning profile
• Seeing every learner's potential for academic success	• Building on a foundation of a quality curriculum	• Basing instructional approaches on student needs and the nature of the content
• Accepting responsibility for maximizing each learner's progress	• Using assessment to inform teaching and learning	• Teaching up
• Recognizing and removing barriers that deny many learners equal access to excellence	• Tailoring instruction to assessment-indicated student needs	• Assigning respectful tasks
	• Leading and managing a flexible classroom	• Using flexible grouping

The Philosophy of Differentiation

Human beings live their lives as works in progress. From early ages, we develop beliefs about a myriad of things. Through our experiences, large and small, we test and refine those beliefs. Few young adults enter parenthood with reliable and robust philosophies of what it means to be able and trustworthy parents. Rather, a fledgling parent becomes more reliable and principled by purposeful reflection on the experience of parenting over time, revised, reinforced, and refined by experience.

Likewise, few teachers enter their initial teaching experience with an informed and tested philosophy of teaching. Instead, the best teachers evolve over time and as a result of critical examination of and reflection about the nature of their work so that, increasingly, their professional decision making is grounded not in habit or compliance or convenience but in a philosophy that acts as a compass pointing them in the direction of true north. In other words, these teachers come to see their practice as representing a set of beliefs that give meaning and purpose to their work beyond that derived from simply executing the duties of a teacher. It is not necessary to have a fully developed philosophy of teaching before attending to student differences in a classroom. With time, experience, and thought, however, it becomes evident that the practice of differentiation is in sync with certain fundamental beliefs about the worth of individuals, what it means to become more fully human, and how teaching and learning can dignify and extend the capacity of teachers and students alike. Differentiation is rooted in and asks practitioners to grow in the ability to dignify human potential. The "philosophy" of differentiation is based on the following essential tenets:

Diversity is normal and valuable. Every life is different from every other one, and every life is of immense worth. We are enriched by the presence of many voices and perspectives in our experiences. Inclusive communities of learners are stronger than exclusive communities.

Every learner has a hidden and extensive capacity to learn. The teacher's key roles are to transmit to the student a belief in the student's ability to achieve (and often exceed) important learning goals, to mentor learners in working hard and working intelligently to achieve important learning goals, and to scaffold growth in learning in a stepwise fashion so that students most often (although not always) experience effort followed by success.

It is the teacher's responsibility to be the engineer of student success. Clearly, students have a primary role to play in their success, as do their families. Nonetheless, it is the teacher's job to enlist and inform students' efforts on their own behalf and to support and encourage families. As one teacher noted, "When someone in my class fails, I've failed too."

Educators should be champions of every student who enters the schoolhouse doors. Arguments abound in other places for and against varied forms of "ability grouping." For purposes of this book, it is sufficient to note that when we segregate students for instruction based on what we perceive they are capable of doing, we have already sent many of them messages that homogeneity matters more than community and that we believe only some students are truly smart. For the students labeled as strugglers, it is difficult not to draw the conclusion that school is a place that is more likely to put them down than to lift them up. For students deemed to be the "smart" ones, segregated classes often come with narrowed worldviews and the high-risk conclusion that people who are smart shouldn't have to struggle. For students classified as "in between," the message seems to be, "You're just average. Although disaster may not befall you in school, it's likely that few real celebratory moments will come your way either." Labels applied to people all too often come with high price tags.

However, it is no more viable to fill classrooms with students whose learning needs are clearly diverse and then teach them as though they are essentially the same than it is to separate students for instructional convenience based on evidence that is inevitably limited. At a time in human history when the world truly is a village and when we need to learn from one another how to live together and solve problems together, classrooms that enable virtually all members of the world community to work successfully together seem a far better alternative. "[In a democracy] education is precisely concerned with equity, access, and recognition of the full humanity of everyone" (Ayres, 2010, p. 138).

Differentiation is a model designed to guide teaching that provides equity of access to excellence for every student. To that end, the teacher in a differentiated classroom believes in the capacity of every student to succeed, works from curriculum that requires every student to grapple with the essential understandings or principles of a discipline and to be a thinker and problem solver in the context of that curriculum, scaffolds the next steps of every learner in a progression toward and beyond critical learning goals, and creates a classroom that actively supports the growth of each of its members.

•   •   •

As you continue to read and think about both your current practice as a teacher and ways in which you aspire to continue your development as a teacher, take time to consider your spoken (and unspoken) philosophy of teaching. How do the tenets of that philosophy manifest themselves in your interactions with students, in your thinking about curriculum, and in your instructional routines? How are the tenets of your current philosophy helpful in your growth as an educator? In what ways might they limit your impact? It is a powerful reality that thoughtful and reflective teaching has the capacity to contribute to the self-actualization of the teacher, just as it can contribute to the self-actualization of the young people with whom that teacher interacts.

3

Rethinking How We Do School— and for Whom

"Just leave me alone to teach my way" is the common mantra. We see the increasing numbers of disengaged students as problems of the students or their families, or of society, not of teachers or schools. It is nigh on impossible to legislate changes to the conception of teaching and learning. . . . So often, the policy changes have little or no effect. The effect of the storm on the ocean is that "the surface is agitated and turbulent, while the ocean floor is calm and serene (if a bit murky). Policy churns dramatically, creating the appearance of major changes . . . while deep below the surface, life goes on, largely uninterrupted."

John Hattie, *Visible Learning*
(quoting from Larry Cuban's *How Teachers Taught*)

Some may think that differentiating instruction is a relatively new idea, hatched from wherever it is that educational "innovations" begin. Actually, its baseline principle is quite old—found in the writings of Confucius and in ancient Jewish and Muslim scriptures: *people differ in their abilities and strengths*. Differentiated instruction simply takes into account those differences.

In more recent history, one-room schoolhouses in the United States, Canada, and other parts of the world practiced differentiation. Six- and 16-year-olds came each day to the same classroom. Teachers planned around the reality that it made little sense to use the same reading book or math problem with everyone in the room, and around the truth that a 16-year-old might require more fundamental mathematics instruction and practice than a 6-year-old. Today, our understanding of what we call differentiated instruction stems from expanded insight into the human brain and how children learn. A brief look at this evolution of knowledge about teaching and learning in recent decades is useful for understanding the foundations of differentiation.

Changes in Education

Think back to what you know of how people lived 75 or 100 years ago. Now, fast-forward to today. In many ways, those years reflect more change for humans than all the prior years of recorded history. For example, think about farming 100 years ago and today. Think about the practice of medicine 100 years ago and today. Consider transportation 100 years ago and today. Consider the 21st century's changes in engineering, entertainment, and communication. The transformation is dizzying! Although many of us succumb to occasional nostalgia for the "good old days," few of us would opt for yesterday's physicians, communication systems, fashions, or grocery stores.

Although we may think of school as a static enterprise—and regrettably, sometimes our practice is static—as educators we understand today many things about teaching and learning that we had no way of knowing a century or even a few decades ago. Some of these insights stem from psychology and the science of the brain. Others come from continuing observation in classrooms. Whatever their genesis, these educational changes are every bit as revolutionary as moving from the pencil to the typewriter to the personal computer—from stone tablets, to paper tablets, to electronic tablets.

Current Knowledge About Teaching and Learning

Our expanding understanding of how children learn, and the implications of this knowledge for teachers, could fill volumes. Capturing all that information is far beyond the scope of this book, but sketching out a few recent, pivotal insights about teaching and learning will enhance our discussion of the differentiated classroom.

Practiced with fidelity to the model, differentiated instruction would always be an outgrowth of our best scientific and experiential insights about teaching and learning, not an end run around them. Our current understanding of learning provides strong support for classrooms that recognize, honor, and cultivate individuality. Following are four contemporary understandings about learners and learning that educators have not always had available to guide their professional practice. All of them are central to the philosophy and practice of differentiation.

Intelligence Is Variable

The study of intelligence over the past half-century points us to the realization that intelligence is multifaceted, not a single entity. Howard Gardner (1991, 1993, 1997) suggests that humans have eight intelligences: verbal-linguistic, logical-mathematical, visual-spatial, bodily-kinesthetic, musical-rhythmic, interpersonal, intrapersonal, and naturalistic—and likely a ninth: existential. That number, of course, has changed from Gardner's initial proposal of seven intelligences. Robert Sternberg (1985, 1988, 1997) suggests three kinds of intelligences: analytical, practical, and creative. Before them, other researchers, such as Thorndike, Thurstone, and Guilford, identified varied types of intelligence. Although the names of intelligences vary, educators, psychologists, and researchers have drawn three significant, consistent conclusions:

- We think, learn, and create in different ways.
- The development of our potential is affected by the match between what we are asked to learn and how we are able to apply our particular abilities to the process of learning.
- Learners need opportunities to discover and develop their abilities in a range of intelligence areas.

The Brain Is Malleable

A powerful and relatively new understanding is that human beings can grow and strengthen our brains just as we can grow and strengthen our muscles. In other words, intelligence is not a characteristic fixed at birth or even solidified in the early years of life. Providing children with rich learning experiences can amplify their ability, and denying them such richness of experience can diminish their intelligence (Caine & Caine, 1994; Dweck, 2000; Sousa, 2010). Neurons grow and develop when they are used actively; they atrophy when they are not used. Vigorous learning literally changes the physiology of the brain (Caine & Caine, 1994; Sousa & Tomlinson, 2011; Sylwester, 1995; Willis, 2010; Wolfe, 2010). It is not the case that we are born "smart" or "not smart" and predestined to live out our days as servants to that reality; rather, we have the capacity to expand our intellectual reach throughout our lives (Dweck, 2000, 2008; Sousa, 2011; Willis, 2010).

These findings have numerous clear implications for educators. Teachers must be effective in recognizing, valuing, and developing many types of intelligence, not just one or two. Students who come to school lacking rich learning experiences can make up lost ground if they find rich experiences in their classrooms. Indeed, all students must continue vigorous, new learning or they risk losing brain power. Key roles for teachers, then, include both ensuring that students are appropriately challenged from their particular points of entry into a given topic of inquiry and helping students understand and become increasingly involved in the attitudes, practices, and habits of mind that contribute to positive brain development.

The Brain Hungers for Meaning

Thanks to progress with imaging technology in the field of medicine, we can now look inside the human brain and see how it functions. Such observations have rapidly expanded the understanding of teaching and learning. We now know important details about what works best for the brain in learning (Caine & Caine, 1994, 1997; Jensen, 1998; National Research Council, 1999; Sousa, 2011; Sylwester, 1995; Wolfe, 2010).

The brain seeks meaningful patterns and resists meaninglessness. Although the brain retains isolated or disparate bits of information, it is much more efficient at retaining information that is "chunked"—organized around categories, concepts, and ideas that increase the information's meaningfulness (National Research Council, 2005). The brain constantly seeks to connect parts to wholes, and individuals learn by connecting something new to something they already understand (Ben-Hur, 2006; Erickson, 2007; Sousa, 2011; Willis, 2006; Wolfe, 2010).

The brain learns best when it can make its own sense out of information rather than when information is imposed on it. The brain doesn't respond much to things that carry only a surface meaning. It responds far more effectively and efficiently to something that carries deep and personal meaning—something that is life shaping, relevant, or important or taps into emotions (Sousa, 2011; Sousa & Tomlinson, 2011; Willis, 2006; Wolfe, 2010).

Brain research tells us much about the individuality of learners and about the nature of effective curriculum and instruction. It tells us that each learner's brain is unique, and educators must provide many opportunities for varied learners to make sense of ideas and information. Research also reminds us that when we set out to have students connect the novel to the familiar, what is novel to one child may already be familiar to another and vice versa (Sousa, 2011; Sousa & Tomlinson, 2011; Willis, 2006).

Our takeaway from this research is that curriculum must cultivate meaning making. It should be organized around categories, concepts, and governing principles. A meaningful curriculum is characterized by high interest and high relevance, and it taps into learners' feelings and experiences. If we want students to retain, understand, and use ideas, information, and skills, we must give them ample opportunity to make sense of or "own" these ideas, information, and skills through involvement in complex learning situations (Sousa & Tomlinson, 2011; Willis, 2010; Wolfe, 2010).

Brain research also strongly suggests that if learning is a process of connecting the unfamiliar to the familiar, teachers must create abundant opportunities for students to link the new with the old. This is a three-part task. First, teachers must identify the essential concepts, principles, and skills of their subjects. Next, they must become experts about their students' learning needs. Finally, they must use this information about learning needs to provide differentiated opportunities for students to construct understanding by connecting what they know with the essentials they are trying to learn (Ben-Hur, 2006; Sousa & Tomlinson, 2011; Willis, 2006).

Humans Learn Best with Moderate Challenge

Through increased understanding of both psychology and the brain, we now know that individuals learn best when they are in a context that provides a moderate challenge (Bess, 1997; Csikszentmihalyi, Rathunde, & Whalen, 1993; Howard, 1994; Jensen, 1998; Sousa & Tomlinson, 2011; Vygotsky, 1978, 1986; Willis, 2006). That is, when a task is far too difficult for a learner, the learner feels threatened and "downshifts" into a self-protection mode. A threatened learner will not persist with thinking or problem solving. On the other hand, a task that is too easy also suppresses thinking and problem solving, encouraging the learner to coast into a relaxation mode.

A task is appropriately challenging when it asks learners to risk a leap into the unknown but they know enough to get started and have support for reaching a new level of understanding. Put another way, both students who consistently fail and those who succeed too easily lose their motivation to learn. For learning to continue, students must understand that hard work is required and have confidence that hard work generally leads to success. Teachers also must remember that what is moderately challenging today most likely won't offer the same challenge tomorrow. Challenges must grow as students grow in their learning (Sousa & Tomlinson, 2011; Willis, 2006).

Again, this new knowledge offers important guidance for educators. What is moderately challenging and motivating for one learner may offer far too little challenge (and therefore little motivation) for a classmate. The same task may be too stressful for yet another classmate. Learning tasks must be adjusted to each student's appropriate learning zone. Further, tasks must escalate in complexity and challenge for students to learn continually.

Thinking About the Students We Teach

There was a time when school was not the diverse mix it is today. Children with physical and severe cognitive challenges stayed home. Children from poor homes, including new immigrants, worked in factories or at other jobs to help support the family. Farm children worked the fields and only attended school during the seasons when crops didn't require planting or harvesting. Girls often were excluded from advanced education because of the perception that their natural role—to marry, raise children, and run a household—did not require much academic study. Children of the very rich often had tutors or went to exclusive boarding schools.

Not too long ago, most children who came to school had two parents at home. At least one of those parents usually was there when the child left for school in the morning and returned in the afternoon. We now teach many children whose homes have only one parent. It's rare that our students have a parent at home at both ends of the school day. Although this fact alone is not necessarily negative, it complicates children's lives. Sometimes children are frightened by this isolation. Many lack a steady hand to monitor school progress or homework—or even to listen to the events of a school day.

We teach children who, for better or worse (and probably both), spend a good amount of time living in cyberspace. Their world is both larger and smaller than that of their parents and grandparents. They know more things but may understand less of what they know. They are accustomed to quick and ready entertainment, yet their imaginations may be less active. They have to cope with realities and problems that once would have been unknown to children, and yet many have markedly smaller support systems for wisely navigating these problems. They are aware of all sorts of positive possibilities in the adult world, but they have little sense of how to build bridges to reach them. These young people are at ease with and itching to use technologies that frighten many of the adults "in charge" of their worlds.

Today, more kinds of children come to school and stay in school, bringing with them a greater range of backgrounds and needs. Many of these children lack the "givens" of early life that a teacher once took for granted. Many are at once enriched and impoverished by their environments. Further, there is a chasm between children who have benefited from enriching childhood experiences and those who haven't had the same opportunities.

The Struggle for Equity and Excellence

In every classroom, no matter the degree of homogeneity, students will inevitably represent a significant range of readiness variance, a broad spectrum of interests, a full complement of approaches to learning, and quite different motivations to learn—or at least to learn the subject being taught. Quite simply, students in any learning context learn better when teachers persistently study their students as people, ascertain the proximity of their students to essential content goals, and use that knowledge to modify instruction in ways that support growth (readiness differentiation), motivation to learn (interest differentiation), and efficiency of learning (learning profile differentiation). The full potential of differentiation, however, is realized when educators understand and draw on its potential to create schools and classrooms that promise equity of access to excellence for the full range of young people whose futures pivot, in large measure, on sustained success with learning and motivation to continue learning.

Too many of today's students come to school from homes where support for academic success is in short supply. Most often this is the case because the parents, although they care deeply about their children, lack savvy about school success or do not have the resources or time to provide the kind of support that would be beneficial. Sometimes students arrive at school without the security provided by parental love. In either scenario, we have children whose immense learning potential is blunted by a lack of the experiences, supports, models, and plans that, if present, would make school success a fundamental expectation of life. On the other hand, many other learners come to school with abundant adult support and with their skills and knowledge months or years ahead of where their learning is expected to be, according to a standard curriculum.

The promise of schools must belong, in equal measure, to all of these children. Educators often speak of equity as an issue for children of the former group and excellence as an issue for the latter. In truth, both equity and excellence must be at the top of the agenda for all children. We cannot achieve equity for children who come to school at risk of falling behind in learning unless we ensure that the best teachers are ready to help them build the sorts of experiences and expectations that the world outside the classroom may have been unable to build for them. We cannot achieve excellence for children at risk of school failure without emphatically, systematically, vigorously, and effectively seeing to the development of their full potential, which implies helping them succeed with dynamic, invigorating curriculum. We must dream big dreams with them and be persistent partners in helping them soar toward those dreams. Both equity and excellence must be a part of our road map for these students.

Children who come to school advanced beyond grade expectations in one or more areas also require equity of opportunity to grow from their points of entry, with teachers doggedly determined to ensure that their potential does not languish. These children need teachers who model, commend, and command excellence—teachers who help them dream big, who cause them to experience, accept, and embrace personal challenge. Both equity and excellence must be a part of our road map for these students, as they must for every learner who comes to us.

Every child is entitled to the promise of a teacher's optimism, enthusiasm, time, and energy, a teacher who will do everything possible, every day, to help students realize their potential. It is unacceptable for any teacher to respond to any group of children (or any individual child) as though the children were inappropriate, inconvenient, beyond hope, or not deserving of focused attention. Providing equity of access to excellence is the great moral challenge of contemporary schools.

Grouping and the Quest for Equity and Excellence

Schools have tried to meet the needs of the full range of learners in one of three ways. First, and most commonly, schools have placed nearly all learners of a given age in a room together where teaching occurs with modest, if any, attention to individual learning needs. Second, schools have separated out students who don't fit the norm because they struggle to learn one or more subjects, know more than the grade-level curriculum asks of them, aren't fluent with the language of the classroom, and so on. These "atypical" students work outside the general classroom for part or all of the school day in special classrooms with similar students whom educators deem to have similar needs. The idea is that, in these settings, teachers can better meet these students at their level of knowledge and skill. In full accord with what common sense would suggest, however, research suggests that, especially for students who struggle with one or more aspects of learning, such homogeneous learning experiences go awry (Gamoran, 1992; Gamoran, Nystrand, Berends, & LePore, 1995; Hattie, 2009, 2012; Oakes, 1985; Slavin, 1987, 1993).

Too often in settings designed to benefit learners whose school performance lags behind grade-level norms, teachers' expectations for the students decline, materials are simplified, the level of discourse is uninspiring, and the pace slackens. When students look around at their peers, they see only other students who are discouraged or who have given up on school. Too few students escape these arrangements to join more "typical" or advanced classes. In other words, remedial classes tend to keep remedial learners remedial (Gamoran, 1992; Gamoran et al., 1995). As van Manen (2003) reflects,

> Once I call a child "a behavior problem," or a "low achiever," or once I refer to him as someone who has a specific learning style, a particular mode of cognitive functioning, then I am immediately inclined to reach into my portfolio of instructional tricks for a specific instructional intervention. What happens then is that I forgo the possibility of truly listening to or seeing the specific child. Instead, I put the child away in categorical language, as constraining as a real prison. Putting children away by means of technical or instrumental language is really a kind of spiritual abandonment. (p. 18)

Some researchers (Allan, 1991; Kulik & Kulik, 1991) suggest that advanced learners who are placed in accelerated, homogeneous classes benefit from a brisk pace, stimulating discourse, raised teacher expectations, and enriched materials. In other words, they continue to advance. These studies, however, compare outcomes for advanced students in homogeneous settings where their learning needs are recognized and addressed with outcomes for advanced learners in heterogeneous settings where their learning needs are *not* recognized and addressed.

There is a modest amount of research on outcomes for students in heterogeneous settings where their learning needs are recognized and addressed. These studies suggest that this latter option can be a viable alternative to homogeneous classes for advanced learners; it is not homogeneity but rather attention to advanced learners' academic needs that matters most (Beecher & Sweeny, 2008; Burris & Garrity, 2008; Rasmussen, 2006; Reis, McCoach, Little, Muller, & Kaniskan, 2011; Tieso, 2002; Tomlinson, Brimijoin, & Narvaez, 2008). In addition, highly selective school settings for high-ability students may actually result in reduced self-concepts for these students, with repercussions for student aspirations and course-taking decisions many years into the future (Marsh, Tautwein, Lüdtke, Baumert, & Köller, 2007; Seaton, Marsh, & Craven, 2010).

In theory, creating academically heterogeneous classes should address equity of access to excellence for all learners simply because of the presence of advanced learners; the full range of learners in the classroom would benefit from the high-level curriculum and instruction designed for advanced learners. There are three major flaws with this assumption, however, at least as schools function to this point.

First, struggling learners will not experience more long-term success by being placed in heterogeneous classes unless teachers are ready and able to meet them at their point of readiness and to systematically escalate learning until these students are able to function as competently and confidently as other learners. Including struggling learners in heterogeneous classes may represent high expectations for all students, but not if students are left to their own devices to figure out how to "catch up" with the expectations. Such an approach does not result in genuine growth for struggling learners.

Another challenge is that in heterogeneous classrooms, advanced students often are asked either to do a greater volume of work than they already know how to do, to ensure the success of other students through much of the school day by serving as peer teachers, or to wait (patiently, of course) while students with less advanced skills continue to work for mastery of content that they themselves have already mastered. Implicitly—and sometimes even explicitly—we suggest that advanced learners are fine without special attention to their needs because they are "up to standards" already. In other words, curricula and instruction in many classrooms tend to be aimed at "average" students and do not account for the nature and needs of advanced learners. This approach clearly can't achieve genuine growth for students whose performance surpasses the aspirations of curriculum designed to teach them what they already know.

A third problem with heterogeneity as it is typically practiced is the assumption that what happens in heterogeneous classrooms for "typical learners" works for virtually all students of a given age. The premise has often been that everyone can benefit from standard, grade-level classrooms. In fact, it is often the case that this standard fare is less than the best we know to do, even for students who perform at or near grade level. Well into the 21st century, heterogeneous classrooms still usually follow a one-size-fits-all approach to teaching and learning, where a standardized learning plan swallows some learners, pinches others, and fails to inspire most. Such an approach provides for neither equity nor excellence for anyone.

By contrast, differentiation offers the possibility of creating effective heterogeneous communities of learning governed by flexible classroom routines that allow and invite attention to students' diverse learning needs. In these classrooms, complex curriculum is the beginning point for instructional planning for virtually all learners, and for all learners there is the possibility for community, equity, and excellence.

What We Know Versus What We Do

Despite compelling new knowledge about learning, how the brain works, and what constitutes effective classroom groupings, classrooms have changed little over the past 100 years. We still assume that children of a given age are enough like each other that they can and should traverse the same curriculum in the same fashion. Further, schools act as though all children should finish classroom tasks as near to the same moment as possible, and that school year should be the same length for all learners.

To this end, teachers generally assess student content mastery via tests based on specific chapters of the adopted textbook and summative tests at the end of designated marking periods. Teachers use the same grading system for all children of a given age and grade, whatever their starting point at the beginning of the year, with grades providing little if any indication of whether individual students have grown since the previous grading period or the degree to which students' attitudes and habits of mind contributed to their success or stagnation. Toward the end of the school year, schools administer standardized tests on the premise that all students of a certain age should have reached an average level of performance on the prescribed content by the testing date. Teachers, students, and schools that achieve the desired level of performance are celebrated; those that do not perform as desired are reprimanded, without any regard to the backgrounds, opportunities, and support systems available to any of the parties.

Curriculum often has been based on goals that require students to accumulate and retain a variety of facts or to practice skills that are far removed from any meaningful context. Drill-and-practice worksheets are still a prime educational technology, a legacy of behaviorism rooted firmly in the 1930s. Teachers still largely run "tight ship" classes and are likely to work harder and more actively than their students much of the time.

To the degree that schools actually focus on developing intelligence, the status quo reflects a belief that only narrow, analytical slices of verbal and computational intelligence are really important. This is almost the same as nearly a century ago, when the public believed that a bit of reading, writing, and computation would serve learners well in an adulthood dominated by assembly-line and agrarian jobs. Schools prepare children for tests more than for life. Sometimes, cartoonists make the point more powerfully than serious prose; see Figure 3.1.

When the lockstep approach to learning does not work well for many children (and it does not), we separate them by what we perceive to be their ability, with virtually no acknowledgment that the instruments and processes we use to sort students are seriously deficient for that purpose and with scant discussion, if any, about the impact labeling and sorting has on either students as individuals or society at large. We then systematically ensure that the most advanced learners get the most experienced and energized teachers and the quality curricula designed to prepare them as thinkers and problem solvers. At the same time, we assign the most vulnerable students to the newest or most discouraged teachers and teach them curricula that require little more than persistent practice of the same low-level, decontextualized skills year after year. After a few years, when the pendulum of attention swings to the awareness that students in the high-level classes are learning more vigorously and successfully than students in the low-level ones,

Figure 3.1 "Another Typical School Day"

CALVIN AND HOBBES © 1993 Watterson. Reprinted with permission of UNIVERSAL UCLICK. All rights reserved.

we shift again to more heterogeneous arrangements but seldom pay diligent attention to addressing students' needs in the "new" settings.

Moving students is not and will not be the solution to creating schools that work for all comers. The solution lies in finding the will to support teacher expertise in creating classrooms where "high-end curriculum" is the standard and differentiation is the mechanism for helping a broad range of students to achieve or even exceed the standards for that level of rigor. Figure 3.2 summarizes what we know to be sound educational practice versus what we often do despite that knowledge. Clearly there are exceptions to the pattern, but the pattern predominates.

Many observers have written wisely and well about why schools seem so resistant to change (Duke, 2004; Fullan, 1993; Fullan & Stiegelbauer, 1991; Kennedy, 2005; Sarason, 1990, 1993). The point here is that whereas many professions have innovated and embraced progress over the last century, the practice of education has remained static.

To align our practice with current best understandings of teaching and learning, we need to begin our investigation of how to differentiate instruction with some important assumptions:

• Students differ in experience, readiness, interest, intelligences, language, culture, gender, and mode of learning. As one elementary teacher noted, "Children already come to us differentiated. It just makes sense that we would differentiate our instruction in response to them."

• To maximize each learner's potential, the teacher needs to meet all students at their own starting points with critical content and ensure substantial growth during each school term.

• Classrooms that ignore student differences are unlikely to maximize potential in any student who differs significantly from the "norm." This is an issue even in "homogeneous" classrooms.

• To ensure maximum student growth, teachers need to make modifications for students rather than assume students must modify themselves to fit the curriculum. In fact, children rarely know how to differentiate their own curriculum successfully.

• Best-practice education should be the starting point for differentiation. It makes little sense to modify practices that defy the best understanding of teaching and learning. As noted educator Seymour Sarason (1990) reminds us, any classroom efforts that aren't powered by an understanding of what keeps children eagerly pursuing knowledge are doomed to fail.

• Classrooms grounded in best-practice education, and modified to be proactively responsive to student differences, benefit virtually all students. Differentiation addresses the needs of both struggling and advanced learners. It addresses the needs of students for whom English is a second language and students who have strong approach-to-learning preferences. It addresses gender differences and cultural differences. It attends to the array of strengths, interests, and approaches to learning that inevitably accompany learners to school. It pays homage to the truths that we are not born to become replicas of one another and that, with intelligent support, all students can accomplish much more than they (or we) dreamed they could. Howard Gardner (1997) reminds us that even if we could figure out how to make everyone a brilliant violinist, an orchestra also needs top-quality musicians who play woodwinds, brass, percussion, and other strings. Differentiation is about high-quality performance for all individuals and giving all students the opportunity to develop their particular strengths. Differentiation

Figure 3.2 Understanding vs. Reality in Education Practice

What We Know	What We Often Do
Students are more diverse today than at any time in our history. Diversity is normal and beneficial.	We tend to see student variance as problematic.
Intelligence is fluid, not static. Virtually all students can learn what is necessary for school success if they work intelligently, diligently, and with strong classroom support.	Schools tend to have a preference for determining which students are smart and which are not in order to separate them for instructional convenience.
Classroom environments that are rooted in strong teacher–student relationships and that build communities of learners have a highly positive impact on student outcomes.	Teachers often feel they have too many students and too many demands to know students well. Classrooms are often collections of individuals rather than teams of learners.
Curriculum should help students understand how the disciplines are organized to make sense, be engaging, focus on student understanding and transfer of knowledge, be relevant to students' lives, and cast them as thinkers and problem solvers.	Curriculum is often dictated by standards, pacing guides, and texts. It rarely connects with students' lives or helps students make sense of the world around them. Emphasis on "right answers" discourages deep thinking and meaning making.
Formative assessment that is used to provide quality feedback, to guide instructional planning, and to develop student autonomy has a powerful impact on student learning.	Formative assessment is often used to give grades and infrequently used to modify instruction in response to varied learner needs. Students infrequently use formative assessment feedback to plan for their own success.
Student differences matter in learning, and attending to those differences is necessary for sustaining learning.	We tend to teach as though all students of a given age are essentially alike.
Instruction that is responsive to student readiness, interest, and approach to learning supports success for more learners.	We tend to persist in one-size-fits-all approaches to teaching, learning, materials, pacing, etc.
Classroom management facilitates growth best when it balances predictability and flexibility, fosters student self-direction, and is built on sound student–teacher relationships.	Classroom management tends to be compliance oriented—rigid, stressing "right answers" rather than the "messiness of thinking," and rooted in distrust of students.
Labeling and sorting students has not proven effective in raising student achievement and carries a significant price in terms of student perception of their own ability and that of others.	We tend to prefer labeling and sorting rather than creating inclusive classrooms designed to ensure that a broad range of students learn and work well together.

supports students in mastering the fundamental competencies and habits of mind and work of successful people that undergird positive outcomes in virtually every area of life.

• • •

At its core, differentiation asks teachers to grapple with a few simple questions. First, why do we assume that children of a given age are "interchangeable" in the way that they learn? What evidence do we have that they come to our classroom with the same skills, knowledge base, attitudes, habits of mind, strengths, inclinations, motivations, confidence level, support system, and approach to school? And without this evidence, why would we ever conclude that it makes any more sense for all of them to learn the same content in the same way and at the same rate than it does for all of them to wear the same shoe size, eat the same amount of dinner, or require the same amount of sleep? The answers to these questions have—or should have—far-reaching implications for how we think about and plan for teaching and learning.

4

Learning Environments That Support Differentiated Instruction

A really good teacher is someone who: knows that a student can teach and a teacher can learn, integrates him[self] or herself into the learning environment, literally taking a seat among the conglomerate of desks, proving that he or she enjoys associating with the minds made of sponges, ready to absorb, appreciates that what one thinks and says is more important than what one uses to fill in the blanks.

Krista, age 17
In Jane Bluestein (Ed.), *Mentors, Masters and
Mrs. MacGregor: Stories of Teachers Making a Difference*

A while ago, a teacher asked me an intriguing question. Her inquiry was earnest, and I responded accordingly, but I have refashioned my answer to her dozens of times since. Her question was, "Is it possible to differentiate instruction in a class where all the students sit in rows and where most of their work is done alone and in silence?"

Her brow was furrowed when she asked the question, and I'm sure mine was furrowed as I replied, "Yes, I think you could apply many principles of differentiated instruction in that setting. You could still offer students appropriately challenging content. You could offer activities at levels that provide moderate challenge for different students. You could offer product assignments that wrap around individual interests and intelligence strengths."

I paused, then added, "You'd have difficulty with students whose approach to learning causes them to itch for collaboration, conversation, and movement." Another pause. "But if I had a choice between a class in which everyone sat silently in straight rows and worked on the same things, in the same way, over the same time spans—or one in which they all sat silently in straight rows and worked on tasks at appropriate degrees of difficulty and with links to their interests—I'd opt for the latter in a heartbeat."

I did go on to say that having only those two options limited both teacher and students. I did not stop in my tracks and say, "Much of what we're talking about here loses its power if the classroom environment is defective."

The teacher who asked the question was "asking between the lines." That is, her words posed only part of her question. She really was saying something like, "OK, I know I have students who come to me at varying points of readiness for my curriculum. I know I'm losing many of them from confusion or boredom. I can even accept that tapping into student interests and learning profiles could help them learn more effectively. I can go along with you on much of that. I don't think I can give up my image of the lady in front of the room who runs a tight ship. You're already suggesting that the way I look at my curriculum should change. Surely you're not asking me to reconstruct my image of myself as a teacher, too!"

I haven't changed my mind about what I said to this teacher. I still think that student tasks should focus on essential understandings and skills. The tasks should be presented in varying ways so all students have to stretch beyond their comfort zone. These kinds of tasks are far preferable to standard-issue work.

I also believe much more about the pervasive importance of classroom environment than I was alert enough to say that day. This teacher was asking me if it makes sense to cure a patient's cold when the patient also has a badly broken leg. Yes, it does. But without a healed leg, the patient still suffers from pain, distress, and a hobbled life.

This chapter contains some of what I could have said to this teacher and explores the essence of differentiated instruction. Children, teachers, and classrooms come together as microcosms of human existence. In unhealthy microcosms, some good things still happen. Great things, however, consistently come from robust, healthy places.

Teaching as a Learning Triangle

I once watched a young, bright, and dedicated math teacher engage in an unspoken battle with his disenchanted students. The teacher's knowledge of geometry was deep and broad. His activities were relevant and intriguing. Yet his adolescent students vacillated between detachment and hostility. What should have been an exemplary class was rife with unspoken animosity. I watched the situation for what seemed an eternity, and I was as happy as the teacher and students when the bell delivered us all from more suffering.

"Why isn't it working?" he asked me later. "What's wrong?" Like many teachers, when I was in the classroom I never had many occasions to explicitly state my beliefs about creating a learning environment. I just taught, day after day, trying to build on what worked and eliminate what didn't. I think my answer to this teacher, however, was an important verbalization of what my students and colleagues had taught me during two decades in a public school classroom.

"Artful teaching is like a learning triangle," I responded. "It's an equilateral triangle with the teacher, the kids, and the 'stuff' at each corner. If any one of these goes unattended and gets out of balance with the others, the artfulness is lost."

This young geometry teacher had problems with two of the legs of the triangle (see Figure 4.1). Although he knew the content thoroughly, he was insecure and didn't have a deep devotion to his kids. As a result, he was a peacock in his classroom, strutting about with a show designed to convince his students (and himself) that he was a hot commodity. A triangle with only one side—a triangle with only the content—isn't a triangle at all.

So that teacher and students together can construct the sort of environment that strengthens the learning triangle, it's important to understand what should happen with, for, and among students, teachers, and the content in a healthy classroom.

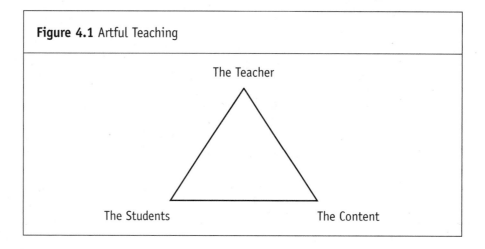

Figure 4.1 Artful Teaching

The Teacher

The Students   The Content

The Teacher: Embracing Classroom Leadership and Responsibility

By its definition, an equilateral triangle is a geometric figure with three equal sides; technically, it has no "top." For our purposes, however, because the teacher is the inevitable leader in any effective classroom, the teacher has to be atop the learning triangle.

Leadership can and should be shared with the learners, but responsibility for the leadership resides with the adult who is charged by professionalism, tradition, and law with that task. Teachers who play this leadership role effectively must be secure about themselves. A teacher who is essentially insecure is unlikely to create a climate of acceptance and affirmation with students, or among students.

That does not mean a secure teacher is free of doubts and uncertainty or is unwavering in direction. Quite the contrary: the variables in a classroom are so great they make uncertainty both inevitable and proper. A secure teacher expects to be a learner all day, every day, and is comfortable with the ambiguity of that role. It's not so important to be "right" as to be open; it's not so important to have all the answers as to be hungry for them. A secure teacher leaves school each day with important questions to puzzle about overnight and the belief that each day contains the insights necessary for a more effective tomorrow. A secure teacher believes that having these kinds of insights is professionally challenging and personally satisfying.

Further, secure teachers accept the reality that they control the climate in the classroom. Their approach to students and instruction determines whether respect, humiliation, delight, drudgery, possibility, or defeat wins the day. They know that they will err some days, but also that they have the capacity and responsibility to avoid the same error another day.

Bob Strachota (1996) reflects on what it means to be a teacher who knows he does not have all the answers—but that he has the power to find them:

> Neither my life in school nor my life away from school is particularly blissful. My car breaks down, I quarrel with my friends, I get sick, and I worry about my children. I have to keep a watch on my moods, needs, biases, weaknesses, and limits in order to see how they are affecting my work. If I can monitor how my emotions are at play in my classroom, I can better put a brake on them when they are destructive, and better allow my joyful, level, nurturant side to dominate. (p. 75)

Strachota's primary goal is to develop his students' capacity to take control of their own lives and learning. He also is aware that he is atop the learning triangle in facilitating that end.

The Students: Attending to Their Differences and Opportunities

Mary Ann Smith is one of my mentors. She doesn't know that, because she moved away from the town where we taught before I had the sense to tell her. She taught primary students when I taught early adolescents, but the essential wisdom she shared with me applies to all learners, whether they're 5 or 55.

Every year, Mary Ann's principal gave her a hefty supply of misfits. I often received those students five or six years later. As I listened to their parents talk, I realized that the only year those youngsters felt comfortable in school was the year they had Mrs. Smith. The mother of four boys, Mary Ann simply created a classroom in much the same way she created her home. Here are some things she knew about kids in both places:

- Each kid is like all others and different from all others.
- Kids need unconditional acceptance as human beings.
- Kids need to believe they can become better than they are today.
- Kids need help in living up to their dreams.
- Kids have to make their own sense of things.
- Kids often make their own sense of things more effectively and coherently when adults collaborate with them.

- Kids need action, joy, and peace.
- Kids need power over their lives and learning.
- Kids need help to develop that power and use it wisely.
- Kids need to be secure in a larger world.

Mary Ann's goal with her own sons—each quite different from the other—was to make them whole, happy, and independent. She adored each boy, as much for his dissimilarities as for his commonalities. She emphasized what each boy did best. She spent time with each child, but they didn't necessarily do the same things. She provided opportunities for each of them, but they weren't always the same opportunities. She monitored their growth, and she provided guidance and discipline in response to their specific needs and issues, not according to a common prescription.

Her classroom was a lot like her home. It was a given that students would differ. She found time for each child at many points during each day. She provided opportunities for everyone's growth and offered guidance as needed. The time she spent with individuals differed in format and content, and the opportunities and guidance differed according to the nature of the dreamer and the dream.

With each child, she looked for strengths and set out to find ways to fortify them. Charlie needed different art materials than some of the others. Eli needed different books to read. Sonja needed to feel the reassuring presence of the teacher to help keep her temper in check. Michelle needed the teacher to remember to "let go" more often.

All these children were dreamers. Mary Ann and her students talked about how they were growing. The students also spoke of how their teacher was proud of all of them for their growth toward their dreams. It was fine that Micah read more than the others, that Philip wiggled and moved around the classroom more, that Chauncie asked unusual questions, that Bess worked first with cubes and then with numbers, that Jorge sometimes asked his questions in Spanish first and then in English. Mary Ann worked from a "growth mindset" (Dweck, 2008), with the conviction that every student had the capacity to learn what mattered and that she could help all of them find and traverse a route to success.

Mary Ann's room was big in heart, options, and support. It was big on content goals and learning standards, but it was short on standardization —and the 8-year-olds understood that just fine. They were not standardized people. They knew it, and, in Mary Ann's classroom, they liked themselves and each other better for that reality.

The Content: Making It Compelling for Learners

A teacher once told me a story about how she came to know what and how to teach in her science class. She had wrestled with curriculum guides that were too long, texts that were too dense or too simple, labs that were sometimes fun but not illuminating, and labs that were neither illuminating nor fun. She watched her students drift away too often, and she felt smothered by what she perceived to be immutable mandates.

A colleague said to her, "Forget all the books and standards for a minute. Go back to what it was that used to make science magic for you. Think about what it used to feel like to do science. Then assume the kids you teach will only have your class to learn about science. It's their only science class—ever. What do you need to teach them so they will love science? Think about that for a minute. Then change one part of what I just asked you to do. Assume you only have three kids to teach: your own three children. And assume that at the end of the year, you will die. What would you teach them about science in that year?"

The teacher said to me, "I've understood what I have to do ever since that day. I don't always know how to do what I have to do, but knowing what I have to do has changed the way I think about what I teach."

Judy Larrick taught English to a group of disenchanted high school students. The curriculum guide required that she teach "classics" that her students found inaccessible and unintelligible. Attendance was down, and Judy's spirits were just as low. Lethargy was the only commodity on the rise. Judy struggled through the year, cheerleading her students and trying to inject energy into essentially dead class periods. The year ended, but Judy didn't berate her students or lament the approach of another year. She went hunting for solutions.

When September came, the curriculum guide was still in place. She still faced a collection of discouraged and irascible adolescents. But as school began, Judy asked, "Anybody here ever been a victim? What does it mean to be a victim? What does it feel like? Can a victim control anything in life? What? When?" A classroom full of "victims" engaged in spirited exchanges. With their teacher, they built a concept map of "victim." Finally, Judy offered, "Want to read a book about somebody else who was a victim, to see whether things play out like you said?" The students read *Antigone* as though they were discoverers of ultimate truth. Class attendance soared and remained high.

Seventh grade teacher Judy Schlimm reflected a similar viewpoint: "My goal as a history teacher is to help my students realize that history is not the study of dead people. It's students holding up a mirror created by the past and seeing themselves in it."

Rachel McAnnallen routinely says to her math students, "Here's the problem we'll be working on. Here's the answer to it. Now, let's talk about all the things that happen or could happen to get us to that answer." The "threat" that often accompanies math leaves the room, and students engage in an eager investigation of possible ways of thinking about a problem.

These four teachers understand the essential purpose of learning. It is not an endeavor that is marked primarily by accumulation of random data, rehearsal of disembodied skills, or checking standards off a list. It is something far more powerful. We are born trying to gain dominion over our environments. We live and die trying to figure out who we are; what life means; how to understand joy, pain, victory, and death; how we must relate to others; and why we are here. The disciplines we study—art, music, literature, mathematics, history, science, or philosophy—give us lenses that help us answer life's ultimate questions. The skills of those disciplines—reading, writing, map making, computing, or illustrating—give us power to use knowledge in meaningful ways (Phenix, 1986). Thinking and puzzling about the unknown gives us far more power than rote regurgitation of isolated names, dates, facts, and definitions or practicing disconnected skills.

The content in a healthy classroom is rooted in these realities. Thus, in a healthy classroom, what is taught and learned

• Is relevant to students, personal, familiar, and connected to the world they know;

• Helps students understand themselves and their world more fully now and as they grow up;

• Is authentic, offering "real" history or math or art, not just exercises about the subject;

• Can be used immediately for something that matters to students; and

• Opens students' ideas to their power and potential both inside the classroom and out in the world.

In a healthy classroom, what is taught welcomes youngsters as reasoning members of the human family, not to a standardized test or to a trivia match. As noted scientist Lewis Thomas (1983) reflects,

> Instead of presenting the body of human knowledge as a mountainous structure of coherent information capable of explaining everything about everything if only we could master all the details, we should be acknowledging that it is, in real life, still a very modest mound of puzzlements that do not fit together at all. (p. 163)

When subject matter is dynamic, intellectually intriguing, and personal —when it bestows power to the learner—the "details" also become more important and memorable. In classrooms established on this belief, students master critical facts and skills, but in the context of and in service of the ideas, issues, problems, and dilemmas that stretch the mind.

Characteristics of a Healthy Classroom Environment

Let's assume we have a teacher who is comfortable with both of her roles as leader and learner in the classroom. She understands and responds to students' essential human needs, and she understands what her subject matter really means for students. What sorts of things would that teacher do to create an environment in which she and her students continually grow in respect and caring for one another? How would she create an environment where subject matter is a catalyst for individual and group growth and appreciation? What does this teacher do to keep the learning triangle dynamic and balanced, to create a true community of learning?

Teaching is a heuristic endeavor, not an algorithmic one. Principles of teaching guide us, but there are no recipes. Following are some characteristics of teaching and learning in healthy classroom environments. They are starting points for reflection, not a complete guide. Feel free to edit the list, to revise it, and to add and subtract from it as you see fit.

The Teacher Appreciates Each Child as an Individual

In *The Little Prince* (Saint-Exupéry, 1943), a young traveler encounters a fox who asks the little boy to "tame" him. When the child is uncertain of the fox's meaning, the fox explains, "One only understands the things that one tames" (p. 70). He explains further that the process of taming takes a long time:

> You must be very patient. . . . First you must sit down at a little distance from me. . . . I shall look at you out of the corner of my eye, and you will say nothing. Words are the source of misunderstanding. But you will sit a little closer to me every day. (p. 70)

The Little Prince comes to understand that through "taming," we learn to see the uniqueness in the thing we tame. "It is only with the heart that one can see rightly. What is essential is invisible to the eye" (p. 73).

The teacher in a healthy classroom works continually to "tame" students in this way: to see who they really are, what makes them unique in the world. There is no such thing as a child who is unattractive. There is no such thing as a child who is "OK" without teacher intervention. The teacher "tames" all comers. Teachers in healthy classrooms also take the risk of allowing their students to know them as people. They take the risk of being "tamed" themselves.

The Teacher Remembers to Teach the Whole Child

In a healthy classroom, the teacher understands that children have intellect, emotions, changing physical needs, cultures, languages, and family contexts. There is a distinction between teaching children about writing or mathematics and teaching mathematics or writing to children. Sometimes emotions must come before the French lesson, and sometimes the French lesson can heal the emotions. A child without self-esteem is often closed to learning, yet genuine accomplishment can produce something more potent than self-esteem: self-efficacy. What children bring to school from home cannot be left outside the classroom door; similarly, for a lesson to be truly powerful, it must go home with the child.

The Teacher Continues to Develop Expertise

Genuine expertise in a subject area is not so much mastery of facts as it is the application of insights and skills. Expert historians do not answer questions at the end of a chapter; they look for new levels of understanding about places, people, and events. A writer does not put words on a page to demonstrate mastery of the rules of grammar. Rather, one writes to find a voice, to uncover meaning in the ordinary and extraordinary stories of life.

Experts use the essential skills and concepts of their disciplines at a demanding, high-quality level. A colleague once remarked to me that the plight of teachers is that we are taught to teach science, not to be scientists. We are taught to teach public speaking, not to be orators.

The Teacher Links Students and Ideas

Poet, novelist, and historical writer Paul Fleischman described how he hoped teachers would use his book, *Dateline: Troy* (1996), which illustrates the events of *The Iliad* with headlines from contemporary newspapers. His comments should spark meaningful reflection among all teachers:

> My real hope is that teachers will be inspired to do what the best teachers have been doing all along—making seemingly remote subjects real and relevant to their students. . . . I think that showing them meaningful links to their own lives will make real readers of them, rather than takers of tests and memorizers of facts. This applies to every subject in the curriculum. Why else did I get a *D* in trigonometry? I was unconvinced that mastering sines and tangents was interesting in its own right or of any practical value to me. I'm confident, however, that the right teacher could convince me. (in Robb, 1997, p. 41)

The Teacher Strives for Joyful Learning

Both words in "joyful learning" are important. In a healthy classroom, the teacher is serious about learning. It is a human birthright to be a learner. There is little we do that is more important. Further, we have too little time for exploring and understanding. Thus, it is essential to focus on what matters most about a subject and ensure that these essentials are at the core of students' experiences.

On the other hand, children are somehow programmed to respond to joy. They are still full of the energy and rhythms of young life. Moving, touching things, laughing, and telling stories are prime entry points for important skills and understandings. Thus, the teacher in a healthy classroom seeks to ensure both engagement and understanding for all learners in every lesson.

A teacher in a summer program for advanced learners left a note on my office door after her fourth day of class. It said simply, "I went for rigor and got rigor mortis." Even highly advanced learners needed joy and challenge, and they made that need abundantly clear to their teacher.

The Teacher Sets High Expectations— and Provides Lots of Ladders

In a healthy classroom, the teacher helps students dream big. Not all of the dreams will be alike, but each student needs to have big dreams and concrete ways to climb to them. Thus, the teacher teaches up. That means knowing quite clearly a child's next learning benchmarks and the scaffolding needed to get there. This may include time lines, rubrics, carefully delineated product assignments, varied working arrangements in the classroom, multiple resources, partnerships with instructional specialists, or small-group remediation or extension.

Every student is worthy of learning the most compelling content available, so the teacher in a healthy classroom begins by thinking about what would interest and challenge the most advanced learners and differentiates to create access for each student to that curriculum. Presenting a robust curriculum with appropriate supports to a broad range of students communicates the teacher's belief in the capacity of each of those students to grow dramatically as learners. Such teaching not only communicates the teacher's growth mindset about a student but also contributes to a learning environment that welcomes, affirms, challenges, and supports each learner in it.

Most young learners don't know how to grow beyond where they are today, until a teacher shows the way. In a healthy classroom, the teacher plays the role of a winning coach, providing a game plan that ensures maximum success for all students from their individual starting points. Then this teacher stays on the sidelines, encouraging, cajoling, and offering advice while every student "plays the game."

The Teacher Helps Students Make Their Own Sense of Ideas

As learners, we seldom "repeat" our way to understanding. Giving back information through a recitation, worksheet, or test seldom produces a learner who retains and uses ideas and information. Many teachers have seen a powerful illustration of this through their own teacher education classes. Because they had no context for what professors were telling them, they often thought the classes were pointless. By the time they were teaching—and had a context for the information—they had forgotten it.

Healthy classrooms are characterized by thought, wondering, and discovery. According to elementary teacher Bob Strachota (1996),

Unless we go through the complexities of struggle and invention, our knowledge is empty. If this is true, I cannot transfer my knowledge and experience to children whom I teach. Instead I have to find ways to help children take responsibility for inventing their own understanding of the world and how to live in it. To do this, I have to struggle against both my training and my instincts which strongly urge me to be directive: to tell children what I know, to tell them what to do. (p. 5)

The Teacher Shares the Teaching with Students

Teachers in healthy classrooms continually invite their students to play a major role in teaching and learning. They do this in a number of ways. First, these teachers help students come to understand and contribute to the operation of a classroom that works for every student. They engage students in conversations about class rules, schedules, and procedures, evaluating with students the effectiveness of processes and routines. When things work well, they celebrate with their students. When processes and routines are not working well, the teacher and students revise and improve them. Second, these teachers ensure that students know to teach one another and learn from one another effectively. Third, these teachers do "metacognitive teaching"; they explain to students—in ways that make sense to young learners—such things as how they plan for classes, what classroom issues they puzzle over when they go home at night, and how they chart progress. Although they accept their leadership role, teachers in these classrooms understand that their students come with vast amounts of tacit knowledge, a clear sense of what works in their world, and valuable insights about themselves and their peers—and with a desire to succeed as learners and as human beings. These teachers build both on students' strengths and on their desire to be active contributors to their world.

In healthy classrooms, there is continual talk about the importance of whatever is undertaken, a consistent sense of urgency about what is to be learned. It isn't a sense of hurriedness but rather a sense that time and topic are valuable and to be treated as such. This involves the same kind of planning as for a promising trip. Teacher and students are full of anticipation as they calculate destinations, map routes, and adjust to new contingencies.

The Teacher Promotes Student Independence

The director of a play has a peculiar job, for weeks orchestrating every move made by various people in a variety of roles, from actors to support personnel. Little happens without the director's intervention in one way or another. When the play opens, however, the director is essentially useless. If the cast and crew can't carry off the play by themselves, the director is a failure.

This is how teaching is, or at least how it ought to be. Every day, teachers should make themselves increasingly useless in their students' lives. Instead of providing solutions, allow students to figure things out for themselves. Provide directions and guidelines for quality, but leave some ambiguity, choice, and flexibility so that students have to make leaps of transfer and apply common sense. Take careful measure of how much responsibility children can manage, making sure to give them that much—and coaching for a bit more as well.

Because there are too many children in most classrooms, teachers often find it easier to do things for students than to contend with the complexities of having them make independent judgments. Teachers often tell me that their 2nd, 5th, or 10th graders are "just too immature to work independently." This leaves me wondering. Can you name the classroom where virtually all students work with high degrees of independence for great chunks of the day? It's kindergarten—peopled by 5-year-olds.

The Teacher Exercises Positive Classroom Management

In healthy classrooms, there is a clear expectation that everyone will deal respectfully and kindly with everyone else. In these places, you hear laughter. Humor and creativity are close kin. Humor stems from making unexpected and pleasurable connections, from freedom to be spontaneous, from the sense that errors can be surprisingly instructive. It is never sarcastic or cutting, and it generates the sort of laughter that stems from the capacity to laugh with others.

Even in the positive and energetic healthy classroom, children need reminders about how to work and how to act; this is necessary to help them grow up to be emotionally and socially sound. In healthy classrooms, however, discipline problems are rarely cataclysmic because students gain attention and power in positive ways. In this context, learners are accepted and valued, and they know it. They are aware that the teacher not only expects great things of them but is their partner in working toward those goals.

In the healthy classroom, students have the opportunity to work and learn in ways that are most comfortable to them as individuals. The teacher provides clear guidelines to help students know how to make appropriate decisions. The teacher ensures that genuine effort on the part of a student results in visible success far more often than not. In this way, the teacher systematically guides learners in becoming captains of their own learning—in understanding the learning goals constructed for them and in setting their own learning goals, in making plans to attain and surpass those goals, in adjusting plans as a situation warrants, in monitoring their own growth, and in deriving energy from the pursuit of quality work.

Such environments eliminate (or at least minimize) many of the tensions that typically lead to misbehavior. When there is a need to deal with a severe or recurring problem, respect for the student, desire for positive growth, and shared decision making result in understanding and learning, not conflict between adversaries.

One summer when I was a child, I found a litter of kittens tucked away in a small space behind an old garage. I nearly burst waiting for my best friend to come home so I could take her to see the wonderful thing I'd discovered. All the way to the kittens, I told her how amazing my surprise was going to be. Between my exuberance and her anticipation, our walking was a cross between toe dancing and flight. When we got to the garage, I stepped back, pointed toward the tiny space, and said, "It's your turn! You go up and see."

A healthy classroom environment feels a lot like that experience, with the teacher continuing to explore for wonderful finds to share. Sometimes we invite individuals to share the journey with us, sometimes a small group, and sometimes the whole class. Whoever we take feels specially chosen, because there is something in the invitation that says, "You are so important that I must show you the treasures I have found!"

The anticipation for this journey is great. The pace is brisk. And then there comes the point where we can step back and say, "I've been there. It's your turn. You think about it your way and see what your eyes make of it. You'll know what to do." Then we watch our students learn, and in the process we become learners too, all over again.

• • •

It's difficult to plan curriculum that grabs the attention of young learners, challenging to think of assessment as a "mentor" rather than a "judge" of learning, demanding to plan instruction that accounts for learner needs, and daunting to guide a classroom that is premised on the need for flexibility. Most difficult of all a teacher's jobs, however, and likely most important in terms of student success, is creating a classroom environment that issues a daily invitation to each learner who inhabits it, offering acceptance, affirmation, challenge, and support.

5

Good Curriculum as a Basis for Differentiation

The Giver flicked his hand as if brushing something aside. "Oh, your instructors are well trained. They know their scientific facts. Everyone is well trained for his job. It's just that . . . without the memories it's all meaningless." "Why do you and I have to hold these memories?" [the boy asked.] "It gives us wisdom," the Giver replied.

Lois Lowry, *The Giver*

A young teacher tried her hand at developing her first differentiated lesson plan. "Could you give it a look and see if I'm on the right track?" she asked me.

Her 4th graders were all reading the same novel. She had fashioned five tasks, and her plan was to assign each student one of the tasks, based on what she perceived to be their readiness levels. She showed me the task options:

1. Create a new jacket for the book.
2. Build a set for a scene in the book.
3. Draw one of the characters.
4. Rewrite the novel's ending.
5. Develop a conversation between a character in this novel and one from another novel they'd read in class that year.

After I looked at the tasks, I asked a question that I wish someone had insisted I answer daily in the first decade of my teaching: "What do you want each student to come away with as a result of this activity?"

She squinted and paused. "I don't understand," she answered.

I tried again: "What common insight or understanding should all kids get because they successfully complete their assigned task?"

She shook her head. "I still don't get it."

"OK, let me ask another way." I paused. "Do you want each child to know that an author actually builds a character? Do you want them all to understand why the author took the time to write the book? Do you want them to think about how the main character's life is like their own? Just what is it that the activities should help the students to make sense of?"

Her face flushed. "Oh my gosh!" she exclaimed. "I don't know. I thought all they were supposed to do was read the story and do something with it!"

"Hazy" Lessons

Many of us could have been this novice. We entered the profession with a vague sense that students should read, listen to, or watch something. Then they should do "some sort of activity" based on it. Consider the following examples:

• A 1st grade teacher reads her students a story. Then she asks them to draw a picture of what they heard. But what should the picture portray? The story's beginning and end? How the main character looked when she was frightened by the stranger? The big tree in the barnyard?

• A 5th grade teacher talks with his students about black holes. Then he shows them a video about the topic. He asks them to write about black holes. To learn what? Why gravity acts as it does in black holes? To deal with issues of time? To demonstrate their understanding of the evolution of black holes?

• As part of a 3rd grade unit on Westward Expansion, students build covered wagons. How does that help them understand exploration, risk, scarcity of resources, or adaptation? Is the activity about pushing frontiers forward—or about manipulating glue and scissors?

• A middle school teacher asks her students to convert fractions into decimals. Is the purpose to get the answers correct and to move on? Or does the teacher have a greater goal in mind: understanding how the conversion works and why it works?

In each example, the teacher had a hazy conception of what children should gain from their experience with content. Students did "something about the story," "something about black holes," "something about Westward Expansion," and a bit of what matters about converting fractions into decimals. Although these activities weren't deadly dull or totally useless, they present at least two problems. One is a barrier to high-quality teaching and learning. The other is a barrier to powerful differentiated instruction.

When a teacher lacks clarity about what a student should know, understand, and be able to do as a result of a lesson, the learning tasks she creates may or may not be engaging and almost certainly won't help students understand essential ideas or principles of the content they are attempting to learn. A fuzzy sense of the essentials results in fuzzy activities, which in turn results in fuzzy student understanding. That's the barrier to high-quality teaching and learning.

This sort of ambiguity also works against differentiated instruction. With most differentiated lessons, all students need to gain the same essential knowledge, use the same essential skills, and probe the same essential understanding. Yet because of variance in their readiness, interests, or approach to learning, students need to master the knowledge, "come at" the ideas, and work with the skills in different ways. Teachers who aren't clear about what all students should know, understand, and be able to do when the learning experience ends have overlooked the vital organizer around which to develop a powerful lesson. That was the problem for the novice 4th grade teacher and her five "differentiated" activities. She just created five "somethings" about the novel. The activities would probably result in five fuzzy understandings about the book—or, more likely, no understanding at all.

This chapter will help reduce the fuzziness that pervades much curriculum and instruction in general. It also sets the stage for the many samples of differentiated instruction in the remainder of the book. The goal is to help you fashion a sturdy foundation for differentiated instruction. After all, creating one version of an activity or product takes time. Creating two or three—and especially five—is more labor intensive. It makes sense to ensure that you have a firm grasp of what makes a solid, powerful lesson before you create multiple versions of it.

Two Essentials for Durable Learning

Over the years, I've been fascinated by how savvy students are about what goes on in classrooms. I have had young adolescents say to me with diagnostic precision, "Her class is lots of fun. We don't learn a whole lot, but it's a fun class." They understand the opposite situation, too: "We're learning math, I suppose, but it always seems like an awfully long class period."

These students voice an implicit awareness that two elements are required for a great class: engagement and understanding. Engagement happens when a lesson captures students' imaginations, snares their curiosity, ignites their opinions, or taps into their souls. Engagement is the magnet that attracts learners' meandering attention and holds it so that enduring learning can occur. Understanding is not just simply recalling facts or information. When learners understand, they have "wrapped around" an important idea, incorporating it accurately into their inventory of how things work. They own that idea.

Brain scientists often use two slightly different terms for the two elements required for enduring learning—meaning and sense. *Meaning* refers to connections between the content and one's own experience and life. *Sense* refers to the learner's grasp of how something works and why. Meaning is a close match for *engagement*, and sense is a close match for *understanding* (Sousa & Tomlinson, 2011). In either case, the message is the same. Students don't really learn if they don't connect with or don't understand the content they study.

A student who understands something can do the following:

- Use it.
- Explain it clearly, giving examples.
- Compare and contrast it with other concepts.
- Relate it to other instances in the subject studied, other subjects, and personal life experiences.
- Transfer it to unfamiliar settings.
- Discover the concept embedded within a novel problem.
- Combine it appropriately with other understandings.
- Pose new problems that exemplify or embody the concept.
- Create analogies, models, metaphors, or pictures of the concept.
- Pose and answer "what if" questions that alter variables in a problematic situation.

• Generate questions and hypotheses that lead to new knowledge and further inquiries.

• Generalize from specifics to form a concept.

• Use the knowledge to appropriately assess his or her own performance or that of someone else (Barell, 1995).

Lessons that are not engaging let students' minds wander. They fail to make the case for relevance because students don't connect the content to what's important in their lives; students have little long-term use for what they might "learn" in such lessons. Lessons that fall short of developing students' understanding of the big ideas or principles that govern the discipline leave students without the capacity to use what they learn in meaningful contexts. Thus, lessons that fall short of engagement and understanding have little staying power and diminish both students' enthusiasm for learning and students' power as learners.

Levels of Learning

Hilda Taba (in Schiever, 1991) understood before many others that learning has several dimensions. We can learn facts, or discrete bits of information that we believe to be true. We can develop concepts, or categories of things with common elements that help us organize, retain, and use information. We can understand principles, which are the rules that govern concepts. The terms *concepts* and *principles* are the more professional terms for what in education we often call "understandings" or "big ideas." As learners, we develop attitudes, or degrees of commitment to ideas and spheres of learning. And, if we are fortunate, we develop skills, which give us the capacity to put to work the understandings we have gained.

Full, whole, and rich learning involves all these levels. Facts without concepts and principles to promote meaning are ephemeral. Meaning without skills needed to translate it into action loses its potency. Positive attitudes about the magic of learning are stillborn until we know, understand, and can take action in our world.

Joan Bauer, author of the young adult novel *Sticks*, speaks of the need for children and adolescents to see connectedness in learning. They need to understand that the principles of science, math, history, and art are the same ones that we find in a pool hall, in our fears, and in the deep wellsprings of courage that make us taller than our nightmares (personal communication, 1997).

In *Sticks*, Bauer displays the skill of a master teacher orchestrating all the levels of learning. She writes of 10-year-old Mickey, who has a fire in his belly to win the 10- to 13-year-olds' nine-ball championship at his grandmother's pool hall. Mickey's father was a pool champ, but he died when Mickey was a baby.

Mickey's friend, Arlen, is as passionate about math as Mickey is about nine-ball. Arlen hasn't memorized math. He thinks mathematically. It is a way of life for him. Math, he explains, will never let you down in this world. Arlen knows what an angle is. He knows that a vector is "a line that takes you from one place to another" (Bauer, 1996, p. 37). These are facts Arlen has learned. Yet he understands the concepts of energy and motion and the principles that govern the concepts, as he explains here:

> "Every body remains in a state of rest or uniform motion in a straight line, unless acted on by forces from the outside. In pool talk, this means a pool ball isn't going anywhere unless it's hit by something, and once it starts moving, it needs something to stop it, like a rail, another ball, or the friction of the cloth on the table." (Bauer, 1996, p. 177)

Because Arlen sees the utility of math, his attitude about math is that it's a language without which many things can't be properly explained. To him, the universe is written in the language of mathematics. What matters most about Arlen, however, is not what he has learned, and not even what he understands. What matters most is his skill. He uses pink yarn to teach Mickey about bank shots and geometric angles, about angles of incidence and angles of reflection. "When you hit the eight ball at a certain angle to the rail, it will bound off the rail at the same angle" (Bauer, 1996, p. 179). Arlen draws diagrams of pool shots so that Mickey sees the lines his balls will draw on the table, but Mickey comes to see much more. He explains:

> "In school I keep seeing the table. Long shots. Short shots. Bank shots. Vectors. I'm seeing geometry everywhere—diamond shaped ball fields, birds flying in V formation. I have grapes for lunch and think about circles. Then I ram the grapes across my tray with my straw. Wham! Two grapes in the corner. It's all connected." (Bauer, 1996, p. 141)

Arlen knew some data. What gave him power, however, was not so much what he knew (facts) but what he understood (concepts and principles) and how he could parlay his understanding into action (skills) in a situation far removed from a schoolhouse worksheet.

All subjects are built upon essential concepts and principles. All subjects, by their nature, call for use of the key skills that professionals in that field use. Some concepts—such as patterns, change, interdependence, perspective, part and whole, and systems—are generic, cut across subjects naturally, and invite linkages. These concepts are a part of physical education, literature, science, computer science—virtually all areas of study. Other concepts are more subject-specific, essential to one or more disciplines but not as powerful in others. Examples of subject-specific concepts include probability in math, composition in art, voice in literature, structure and function in science, and primary source in history.

Similarly, skills can be generic or subject-specific. Generic skills include writing a cohesive paragraph, arranging ideas in order, and posing effective questions. Skills that are subject-specific include balancing an equation in math, transposing in music, using metaphorical language in literature and writing, and synthesizing sources in history. Figure 5.1 illustrates the key levels of learning in several subject areas.

During planning, a teacher should generate specific lists of what students should know (facts), understand (concepts and principles), and be able to do (skills) by the time the unit ends. Then the teacher should create a core of engaging activities that offer varied opportunities for learning these essentials in contexts that connect with the world of the learner. Activities should lead a student to understand or make sense of key concepts and principles by using key skills. In later chapters of this book, illustrations of differentiated lessons typically are based on specific concepts, principles, facts, and skills that ensure this kind of clarity.

Addressing Standards in a Meaningful Way

In many districts, teachers feel great pressure to ensure that students attain standards delineated by the district, the state, a particular program, or a professional group. Standards should be a vehicle to ensure that students learn more coherently, more deeply, more broadly, and more durably. Sadly, when teachers feel pressure to "cover" standards in isolation, or when the

Figure 5.1 Examples of the Levels of Learning in Different Content Areas

Levels of Learning	Science	Literature	History
Facts	• Water boils at 212° Fahrenheit. • Humans are mammals.	• Katherine Paterson wrote *Bridge to Terabithia*. • Definition of *plot* and definition of *character*	• The Boston Tea Party helped to provoke the American Revolution. • The first 10 amendments to the U.S. Constitution are called the Bill of Rights.
Concepts	• Interdependence • Classification	• Voice • Heroes and antiheroes	• Revolution • Power, authority, and governance
Principles	• All life-forms are part of a food chain. • Scientists classify living things according to patterns.	• Authors use voices of characters as a way of sharing their own voices. • Heroes are born of danger or uncertainty.	• Revolutions are first evolutions. • Liberty is constrained in all societies.
Attitudes	• Conservation benefits our ecosystem. • I am part of an important natural network.	• Reading poetry is boring. • Stories help me understand myself.	• It's important to study history so we write the next chapter more wisely. • Sometimes I am willing to give up some freedom to protect the welfare of others.
Skills	• Creating a plan for an energy-efficient school • Interpreting data about costs and benefits of recycling	• Using metaphorical language to establish personal voice • Linking heroes and antiheroes in literature with those of history and current life.	• Constructing and supporting a position on an issue • Drawing conclusions based on analyses of sound resources

Continued

Figure 5.1 Examples of the Levels of Learning in Different Content Areas *(continued)*

Levels of Learning	Music	Math	Art	Reading
Facts	• Strauss was known as "the Waltz King." • Definition of *clef*	• Definition of *numerator* and *denominator* • Definition of *prime numbers*	• Monet was an Impressionist. • Definition of *primary colors*	• Definition of *vowel* and *consonant*
Concepts	• Tempo • Jazz	• Part and whole • Number systems	• Perspective • Negative space	• Main idea • Context
Principles	• The tempo of a piece of music helps to set the mood. • Jazz is both structured and improvisational.	• Wholes are made up of parts. • The parts of a number system are interdependent.	• Objects can be viewed and represented from a variety of perspectives. • Negative space helps spotlight essential elements in a composition.	• Effective paragraphs generally present and support a main idea. • Pictures and sentences often help us figure out words we don't know.
Attitudes	• Music helps me to express emotion. • I don't care for jazz.	• Math is too hard. • Math is a way of talking about lots of things in my world.	• I prefer Realism to Impressionism. • Art helps me to see the world better.	• I am a good reader. • It's hard to "read between the lines."
Skills	• Selecting a piece of music that conveys a particular emotion • Writing an original jazz composition	• Using fractions and decimals to express parts and wholes in music and the stock market • Showing relationships among elements	• Responding to a painting with both affective and cognitive awareness • Presenting realistic and impressionistic views of an object	• Locating the main idea and supporting details in news articles • Interpreting themes in stories

standards are presented in the form of fragmented and sterile lists, genuine learning is hobbled, not enriched.

Every standard in a prescribed list is a fact, a concept, a principle (understanding), an attitude, or a skill. Some standards *imply* more than one level of learning. It is a valuable exercise for teachers, administrators, and curriculum specialists to review standards and label each of the components with its level of learning—and then "unpack" the standards, with multiple implicit levels of learning embedded.

Some sets of standards are based on concepts and principles, integrating skills of the particular discipline into networks of understanding, as is the case with many of the standards developed by high-level professional groups. In other instances, however, standards reflect predominantly skill-level learning, with an occasional knowledge level, and less frequently a principle level, included. When this is the case, educators need to fill in the blanks, making certain that learning experiences are solidly based on concepts and principles and that students use skills in meaningful ways to achieve or act upon meaningful ideas.

This point hit home for me when I heard one educator telling another about a classroom she had visited. "I asked the child what the class was working on," the educator reported. "She told me they were writing paragraphs, and I asked what they were writing about. She told me again that they were writing paragraphs. I wrinkled my brow and asked, 'But why are you writing the paragraphs? What are you trying to communicate?' She answered me with some irritation, 'Oh, that doesn't matter in here. We're just writing paragraphs!'"

Contrast the mechanical way in which this teacher is "teaching" students standards about writing with another teacher who took a more meaningful approach to ensuring that students became proficient with standards—in this case, to understand how particular elements in fiction interact (for example, how setting shapes plot or characters).

Realizing that the standard as stated was disconnected from her middle school students' experiences, she first had students talk about elements in their own lives and how these affected one another. They discussed how music influenced their mood, how they could be swayed by friends, how the time of day impacted their energy level, and so on. She moved from that to helping students discover that the stories they had enjoyed reading worked the same way: authors use elements like the motivation of a character (to drive the action in a story) or the weather (to help readers understand a character's mood). Students suggested some principles about how elements in systems interact in life and in fiction. They tried out their ideas about the interaction of elements in songs they cared about, in movies they'd seen, and in art and photography—and then refined these principles as their conversations about the writer's craft developed over time. This teacher's students found the exploration to be not only worth their time and participation but also very helpful with their own writing. Many of them even commented on interaction among elements in fiction and interaction among elements in the scientific and governmental systems they were studying in social studies class.

Put another way, teaching information and skills without connection to and use in addressing coherent, meaning-rich ideas is hollow. In addition, as was discussed in Chapter 3, teaching mechanics without meaning is counter to the way humans learn.

Standards are an important part of a curriculum, but they should not be seen as "the" curriculum. They are ingredients in curriculum in the same way that flour, yeast, water, tomato sauce, and cheese are ingredients in pizza. It's a foolish cook who assumes diners who are asked to eat two cups of flour, a cup of water, a tablespoon of yeast, an eight-ounce can of tomato sauce, and a block of cheese will feel they have had a tasty pizza. It's a foolish teacher who confuses ingredients with an inviting and wholesome learning experience.

Learning Levels: A Case in Point

I remember watching two 3rd grade teachers scramble to figure out how they could "cover" another unit in science before the year ended. They told me they had "moved too slowly"; they still had to "do" clouds with students in the few remaining days of class.

The two teachers worked hard to lay out materials from science books, which they would have their students read. They found some stories about clouds that students usually liked with the hope that they'd have time to read them. The two teachers agreed on cloud worksheets the students could complete, and they chose an art activity the students would enjoy. All this work seemed very urgent and purposeful. Yet as the two began to decide the order in which they'd use the materials, one teacher discovered she had forgotten the name of one kind of cloud. The second teacher realized she recalled the names, but she couldn't match the names to any pictures. Both teachers had "taught the cloud unit" several times.

This example of "planning a unit" is common. With good intent, teachers try to do what their program of study outlines. In this case, the outline said students should know and recognize different kinds of clouds. Although the curriculum guide may have stated how this segment of study fits into a larger framework of understanding and skills, the guide did not make that explicit to the teachers, who, in turn, would not make it explicit to their students. Because the unit these teachers prepared was largely fact-based and devoid of understandings (concepts and principles) and skills, it is not surprising that the teachers themselves had difficulty recalling the facts. This did not portend rich, long-term outcomes for their students.

By contrast, another teacher mapped out her whole year in science around four key concepts: change, patterns, systems, and interrelationships. Throughout the year, students examined a range of scientific phenomena, learning how these illustrated the four concepts. At the outset of each exploration, the teacher identified the essential principles she wanted all students to grasp through their study. Some of the principles were repeated in several units. For example, natural and human-made things change over time. Change in one part of a system affects other parts of the system. We can use patterns to make intelligent predictions. Some understandings, on the other hand, were specific to a particular study (e.g., water continually changes in form, but its amount does not change). The teacher also created a list of skills students were to master in the course of the year. Her students needed to learn to use particular weather tools, to make predictions based on observations rather than guesses, and to accurately communicate through pictures and written statements. At appropriate places in their various studies, students used the skills to understand key principles. Facts were everywhere as students talked about specific events just as scientists would.

At one point in the year, students used weather instruments (skills) to talk about patterns and interrelationships in weather systems (concepts). They explored two principles: (1) change in one part of a system affects other parts of the system, and (2) people can use patterns to make intelligent predictions. Then they predicted (skill) what sorts of clouds (facts) would be likely to form as a result of the patterns and interrelationships they saw. They illustrated and wrote about their predictions using appropriate cloud terminology. They then observed what happened, assessed the accuracy of their predictions, and communicated their observations in the form of revised drawings and explanations.

This kind of planning for student learning creates a structure for coherent understanding all year. Facts illustrate and cement key ideas that are redis-covered repeatedly. Skills have a purpose rooted in meaning and utility, and learning promotes both engagement and understanding. These students are more likely to understand how their world works and to feel more competent as learners and young scientists. They also are more likely to remember the names and nature of clouds in years to come—and so is their teacher.

Curriculum Elements

To ensure effective teaching and learning, teachers need to link tightly three key classroom elements involved in learning: content, process, and prod-uct. (The other two elements are learning environment and affect. Those elements were introduced in Chapter 3, and they must consistently remain central to thinking about, planning for, observing, and assessing instruction.)

Content is what a student should come to know (facts), understand (concepts and principles), and be able to do (skills) as a result of a given segment of study (a lesson, a learning experience, a unit). Content is input. It encompasses the means by which students will become acquainted with information (through textbooks, supplementary readings, web-based doc-uments, videos, field trips, speakers, demonstrations, lectures, computer programs, and a host of other sources).

Process is the opportunity for students to make sense of the content. If we only tell students something and then ask them to tell it back to us, they are highly unlikely to incorporate it into their frameworks of understanding. The information and ideas will belong to someone else (teacher, textbook writer, speaker). Students must process ideas to own them. In the classroom, process typically takes place in the form of activities. An activity is likely to be effective if it

- Has a clearly defined instructional purpose;
- Focuses students squarely on one key understanding;
- Causes students to use a key skill to work with key ideas;
- Ensures students will have to understand (not just repeat) the idea;
- Matches the student's level of readiness; and
- Helps students relate new understandings and skills to previous ones.

A *product* is the vehicle through which students show (and extend) what they have come to understand and can do as a result of a considerable segment of learning (such as a month-long study of mythology, a unit on weather systems, a marking period spent on studying governments, a semester learning to speak Spanish, a year's investigation of ecosystems, or a week focusing on the geometry of angles). The examples in this book use the term to signify a culminating product, or something students produce to exhibit major portions of learning, not the pieces of work students routinely produce during the course of a day to make their thinking evident. For the purposes of this book, those short-term creations simply are concrete and visible elements of an activity.

A culminating or summative product might take the form of a demonstration or exhibition. Students could design a solution to a complex problem or undertake major research and written findings. A culminating product can be a test, but it just as easily can be a visual display such as a narrated photo essay. In other words, a product can be a paper-and-pencil assessment, a performance assessment, or a project. Whatever the type, culminating products

• Tightly align with the knowledge, understanding, and skill that are clear to the teacher and students throughout the period being assessed;

• Emphasize student understanding rather than repetition of knowledge or algorithmic use of skills; and

• Are accessible to students with a range of learning needs (e.g., vision, reading, writing, attention, language problems).

Culminating products that take the form of performance assessments or projects should also

• Clearly define what students should demonstrate, transfer, or apply to show what they know, understand, and can do as a result of the study;

• Provide students with one or more modes of expression, which may include the opportunity for a student to propose a format, as long as the learning outcomes to be demonstrated remain constant;

• Communicate precise expectations for high-quality content (information gathering, ideas, concepts, research sources), steps and behaviors for developing the product (planning, effective use of time, goal setting, originality, insight, editing), and the nature of the product itself (size, audience, construction, durability, format, delivery, mechanical accuracy);

• Provide support and scaffolding (e.g., opportunities to brainstorm ideas, rubrics, time lines, in-class workshops on use of research materials, opportunities for peer critiques and peer editing) for high-quality student success; and

• Allow for meaningful variations in student readiness, interest, and learning profile.

Joining Learning Levels and Curriculum

Effective teachers ensure that the unit or segment they are exploring with their students addresses all levels of learning. They make certain to build activities so that the content, process, and product incorporate materials and experiences that will lead students to engage with and genuinely understand the subject. This means that content, process, and product are squarely focused on exploring and mastering key concepts, essential principles, related skills, and necessary facts (see Figure 5.2).

For example, Ms. Johnson and her middle schoolers will soon undertake a study of mythology. The concepts she and her students will explore in this study (and throughout the year) include hero, voice, culture, and identity. The principles they will investigate include the following:

• People tell stories to clarify their beliefs for themselves and others.
• Our stories reflect our culture.
• Understanding someone else's worldview helps us clarify our own.
• When we compare the unfamiliar with the familiar, we understand both better.
• Who a person or culture designates as hero tells much about the person or culture.
• Myths are mirrors of values, religion, family, community, science, and reasoning.

The skills that will be emphasized in the month-long study include synthesizing text, comparing and contrasting, interpreting and using similes and metaphors, abstracting themes from fiction, and supporting ideas with text. As is the case throughout the year, Ms. Johnson will make certain students use the vocabulary of fiction (*plot, setting, protagonist, antagonist, tone*) as

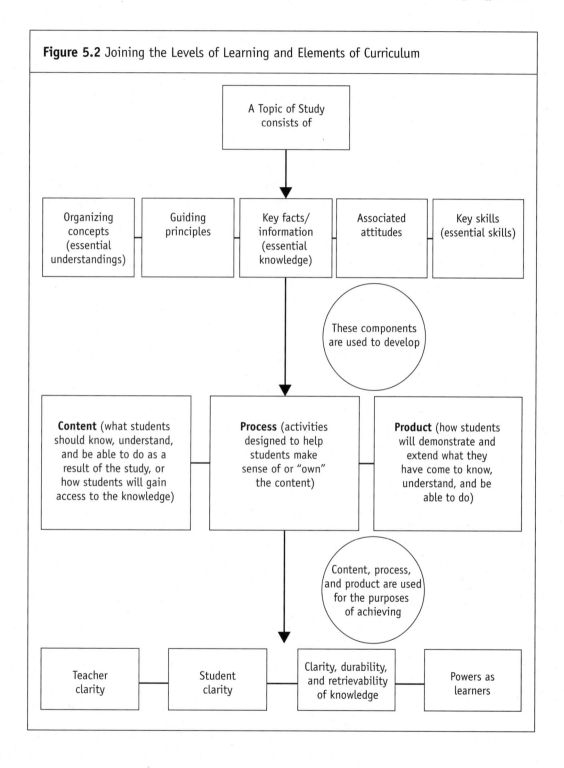

Figure 5.2 Joining the Levels of Learning and Elements of Curriculum

they talk about and work with the myths. Ensuring that students encounter characters and events (facts) from key myths often and in various contexts will familiarize them with important names and events that contribute to the vocabulary, symbols, and allusions in their own and other cultures.

Knowing the key facts, concepts, and principles she intends her students to learn directs Ms. Johnson's selection of myths (content). She knows, for example, that she must select myths from several cultures; include clear exemplars of heroes; reveal views about religion, community, and science; and introduce events and characters that are the basis for often-used cultural symbols and allusions.

Ms. Johnson develops core activities (process) to help students link what they read and talk about from the myths with their own cultures, beliefs, and ways of thinking. The activities will require students to use targeted skills, and she plans to directly teach these skills as needed. For example, she and her students will explore the idea of a "hero" as presented in Greek, Norse, African, and Inuit myths. For one sense-making activity, she's considering having students write (and perhaps present) a conversation between a mythological hero and a contemporary hero on a theme that is relevant to both times and cultures. This activity will require students to compare and contrast the heroes' cultures and beliefs. To do so, they will have to know important characters and events, understand the concept of hero, apply the principles they've been studying, and use the skill of synthesizing text. They will use excerpts from myths to guide development of their conversations.

For a culminating product, Ms. Johnson plans to offer several options, all of which require students to

• Demonstrate their understanding of myths as mirrors of the concept of hero and culture;

• Use core knowledge about important characters and events from important myths; and

• Use the targeted skills of understanding theme, metaphorical thought and language, synthesizing text, comparing and contrasting, and using text to support ideas.

Ms. Johnson's clarity about what students must know, understand, and be able to do as a result of a unit promotes both student engagement and student success. Students see ancient myths as very much like their own lives. The myths make sense, seem real, and connect to things they feel are important. The myth unit will promote understanding by linking new knowledge and insight with the familiar. As Ms. Johnson and her students explore myths, she will teach them to use appropriate terms and skills in discussions and writing so that they connect knowledge, understanding, and skills into a meaning-rich whole.

These types of activities help students build frameworks to organize, think about, apply, and transfer knowledge, skills, and ideas. They provide reinforcing and connective learning opportunities through all elements of the curriculum. Ms. Johnson has not yet started to think about differentiating instruction for varied student readiness levels, interests, and approaches to learning. However, she is laying the foundation for doing so in a rich and meaningful way.

The Curriculum–Assessment–Instruction Connection

It seems little more than common sense that teachers who care deeply about both their students and their subject, and who invest heavily in both, would be vigilant in determining where students are at a given time relative to critical learning goals. Common sense, of course, can be uncommonly difficult to achieve, as habits, desires, and other distractions cause us to function in less than logical ways.

A sensible cycle in teaching would be to set clear goals for a unit of study, develop tentative plans to help students master those goals, check to see where students are relative to those goals prior to beginning instruction, adapt the tentative plans based on what is learned about students' needs, teach the first segment of content with both the goals and students' needs in mind, check to determine student grasp of the content in the first segment, adapt plans for the next segment based on what is learned about student progress, and so on.

Sadly, the pattern many of us follow in school is often more like this: decide what to teach first, teach it; decide what to teach next, teach it; decide what to teach third, teach it; and so on. At one or more "concluding" points in the cycle, we give a test so that there's something to record in the grade book. Then we repeat the cycle. Despite the prevalence of this progression, when we teach this way we've abdicated the essence of effective teaching. Effective differentiation depends on

- Teacher and student clarity about what students should know, understand, and be able to do as the result of any segment of learning;
- Teacher and student clarity about where the student is relative to those goals at a given time; and
- The teacher's acceptance of responsibility to ensure that subsequent segments of learning deal directly with student gaps, misunderstandings, and advanced mastery in ways that are highly likely to promote significant growth.

In other words, goal clarity informs design of pre-assessments and formative assessment, which in turn inform teacher understanding of students' points of learning, which in turn informs teacher instructional planning. Formative assessment and pre-assessment can incorporate both formal and informal measures of student readiness, interests, and approaches to learning. The alignment of clear curricular goals, ongoing assessment, and instruction drives meaningful differentiation.

•   •   •

Fundamentally, differentiation is an instructional model focused on *how* teachers teach and *how* students learn in a classroom—not on *what* teachers teach or *what* students learn. The "what" is a curricular issue. So it would seem that a model of differentiation would be unconcerned with the nature of curriculum. But, of course, teachers have to differentiate "something," and the quality of that "something" will certainly affect both the power of the differentiation and the quality of the student experience in the classroom. If a curriculum is all "drill and s(kill)," it likely still makes sense to differentiate that curriculum, but consider how much more potent the curriculum, the instruction, and the learning could be if students learned those skills in pursuit of solutions to authentic dilemmas or problems encountered by adults in their jobs or avocations. Consider, too, that if a teacher differentiates even a promising curriculum but lacks clarity about its essential knowledge, meaning, and skills, the differentiation will offer students multiple pathways into fog.

Curriculum ought not be thought of as a document or program teachers teach "as is" but rather as a starting point for helping learners make sense and meaning of the world they inhabit. Much of the art of teaching resides in the capacity to integrate required content outcomes into coherent learning experiences that capture young imaginations, build reliable organizational frameworks in young brains, and ensure that learners learn deeply what matters most in the disciplines they study.

6

Teachers at Work Building Differentiated Classrooms

Students do not simply store knowledge they hear; each student learns in a particular, personal way. Each child gives personal shape to his or her understanding and to the way that he or she comes to understand things. . . . The teacher may be teaching a class of 35 students; but it is always important to remember that all learning is ultimately an individual process.

Max van Manen, *The Tact of Teaching*

Teachers in the most exciting and effective differentiated classes don't have all the answers. What they do have is optimism and determination. They are dogged learners who come to school every day with the conviction that today will reveal a better way of doing things—even if yesterday's lesson was dynamite. They believe they can find this better way by aggressively searching out and examining the clues implicit in what they do. This conviction guides all aspects of their work, every single day.

These teachers shun "recipe" teaching. They know that even if they do filch an idea from someone else's stores (a time-honored and defensible practice among teachers!), they must adapt it for their own learners' needs, fit it to essential learning goals in their own classroom, and polish it so it becomes a catalyst for engagement and understanding among their own students. Longtime teacher Susan Ohanian (1988) expands on this point, drawing on Confucius's admonition that someone can reveal to us "one corner" of understanding, but we must find the other three ourselves:

> I know plenty of teachers who are disappointed, indignant, and eventually destroyed by the fact that nobody has handed them all four corners. . . . It is up to us to read the research and to collaborate with the children to find the other three corners. And because teaching must be a renewable contract, if we don't keep seeking new understanding, we'll find that the corners we thought we knew very well will keep slipping away. There are constant, subtle shifts in the schoolroom. One can never be sure of knowing the floor plan forever and ever. (p. 60)

Chapters 6, 7, and 8 offer examples of differentiated curriculum and instruction to illustrate the key principles of differentiation (see Figure 6.1). Please note that these are not ready-made lessons to be transported into other classrooms; they simply reveal one corner of the differentiation process. The success of the teachers profiled rests on their developing and maintaining a learning environment that invites students to do the hard work of learning and consistently supports them in that journey. The other keys to their success include compelling curriculum with clearly articulated learning goals that are centered on student understanding, persistent assessment that aligns precisely with designated learning goals and informs teacher understanding of student development toward and beyond critical goals, and instructional planning that is responsive to both students' needs and content requirements.

Figure 6.1 Key Principles of a Differentiated Classroom

- An invitational learning environment is pivotal in student achievement.
- Quality curriculum provides the foundation for powerful differentiation.
- Formative assessment informs teaching and learning.
- Instruction is based on formative assessment information and responds to readiness, interest, and learning profile needs.
- Teacher leadership and flexible classroom routines prepare students to understand, contribute to, and succeed in a differentiated environment.

The examples also illuminate the heuristic thought processes of these teachers and their approach to differentiating instruction. This is intended to support you, as a teacher, in your search for the "other three corners" with your particular students, in your particular subject areas, and according to your particular personality and your needs as an educator and a human being.

Differentiating: The What, How, and Why

There are three questions that are very useful in analyzing differentiated curriculum and instruction: *What* is the teacher differentiating? *How* is the teacher differentiating? *Why* is the teacher differentiating?

What is the teacher differentiating? This question focuses us on the curricular element the teacher has modified in response to learner needs. It might be one or more of the following:

• Content—what students will learn or how the students will get access to the information, skills, and ideas that are essential to understanding and using those elements;

• Process—the activities through which students make sense of key ideas using essential knowledge and skills;

• Product—how students demonstrate and extend what they know, understand, and can do as a result of a segment of learning; or

• Affect/learning environment—the classroom conditions and interactions that set the tone and expectations of learning.

How is the teacher differentiating? This question focuses us on the student trait to which the differentiation responds. Is the teacher differentiating in response to student readiness, interest, learning profile, or some combination of the three? Any learning experience can be modified to respond to one or more of these student traits.

Why is the teacher differentiating? Here, we consider the teacher's reason for modifying the learning experience. Is it to support access to learning? To increase student motivation to learn? To improve the efficiency of learning? Any or all of these three reasons for differentiating instruction can be tied to student readiness, interest, and learning profile.

Students can't learn that which is inaccessible to them because they have no way to understand it. They can't learn when they are unmotivated by material that is consistently too difficult or too easy. We all learn more enthusiastically those things that connect to our interests and experiences; we learn more efficiently if we can acquire information, practice skills, make sense of ideas, and express our understanding through a preferred mode.

Some of the examples of differentiation that follow reflect modest, though important, modifications of curriculum and instruction. Others are more elaborate. Each section is followed by an analysis of what the teacher was thinking in planning this response to student needs—the what, how, and why. You might find it interesting to do your own analysis before reading the one provided. In Figure 6.2, you'll find a reminder of the three key questions and the elements to consider.

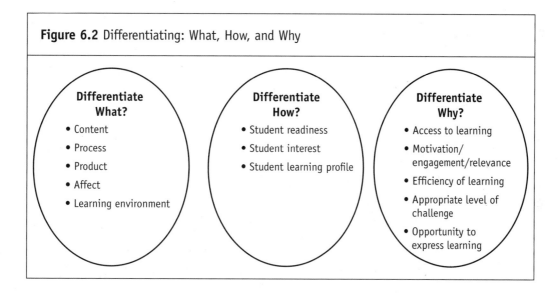

Figure 6.2 Differentiating: What, How, and Why

Differentiate What?
- Content
- Process
- Product
- Affect
- Learning environment

Differentiate How?
- Student readiness
- Student interest
- Student learning profile

Differentiate Why?
- Access to learning
- Motivation/engagement/relevance
- Efficiency of learning
- Appropriate level of challenge
- Opportunity to express learning

Differentiating Fact- or Skills-Focused Instruction

Consistently teaching skills in isolation can strip learning of relevance and power. Yet there are times in most classes when teachers appropriately opt to have students practice with facts or with a specific skill. In good scenarios, teachers then ask students to complete meaning-rich tasks or knotty problems using the information or skills, introducing the more meaningful tasks or problems prior to the practice so students can see purpose in the more rote work they are asked to do.

Because in any class, student readiness for particular information or skills is varied, teachers need to differentiate how students practice those elements.

Here are some examples of teachers differentiating fact- or skills-focused assignments based on their assessment and understanding of students' points of entry.

Grade 1 Science: Classification

Yesterday, Mrs. Lane's 1st graders took a nature walk to gather objects they could think about as scientists might. Today, they will work in groups to classify the items they found on their walk.

All students will first classify items as living or nonliving. Then, within those categories, students will classify by other similarities (such as shape, size, color, and type of object). Mrs. Lane has made one adaptation at several tables. Some of the younger 1st graders will classify only the actual objects. At other tables, she has replaced some of the objects with cards that bear the object's name. This is for early readers excited about their newly evolving skill. Based on their readiness to decode the object names, several of the early readers have one or two cards, and others have many.

Differentiating what? The task as a whole enables students to practice and make sense of what it means to compare and contrast. Mrs. Lane is differentiating process.

Differentiating how? She is differentiating process based on her ongoing assessment of students' reading readiness.

Differentiating why? Mrs. Lane wants her young readers to have as many chances as possible to use their reading skills. The word cards also help nonreaders; when students at the various tables share how they classified the items, the nonreaders encounter examples of object–word connection, which is essential to learning to read.

Grade 4 Language Arts: Proofreading

Mr. Mack's 4th grade classroom includes a learning center designed to support students in refining their ability to detect and correct errors in punctuation, spelling, and sentence structure. The proofreading center has a collection of stories that Mr. Mack has written to engage students at different reading levels. Sometimes students find messages from characters in stories they are reading, from people in current events, from Mr. Mack himself, or from the gnomes and trolls Mr. Mack declares inhabit the classroom's crannies to observe what goes on. Mr. Mack, of course, writes these pieces with humor, a dash of wisdom, and different types of errors, depending on which students will be called upon to edit them. The complexity of the prose varies as well.

At other times, students leave their own writing in an in-box at the proofreading center so peers can help them polish their drafts. Mr. Mack screens these pieces too, asking particular students to review certain papers, which he knows they can respond to in a meaningful way based on the author's needs and the reviewer's proficiency.

Differentiating what? Skills-based practice is the focus of teacher assessment. Mr. Mack differentiates the process so that the particular punctuation, spelling, and sentence structure requirements are a good match for students' skill needs. At the same time, he is ensuring appropriately challenging reading readiness levels. In both instances, he is differentiating content.

Differentiating how? Mr. Mack's differentiation is based on readiness, which in this case targets proficiency in punctuation, vocabulary, and sentence structure. Keenly aware of student interests, he has a great time dashing off error-ridden notes from book characters, sports heroes, or gnomes, knowing these notes will strike a chord with particular learners. In addition, he matches topics of student writing with reviewer interest whenever he can. The approach works. Students look forward to proofreading in Mr. Mack's class.

Differentiating why? Mr. Mack's students have different skill needs in writing and proofing. Varying the errors in the materials he prepares provides an efficient way to move students along the skills continuum as quickly as possible. He also avoids undue boredom from unnecessary repetition of previously mastered skills and circumvents the confusion that occurs when the skills called for are beyond a student's readiness. His awareness of student readiness related to spelling, sentence structure, and punctuation allows him to convene various small groups for direct instruction on particular skills, and he can bring together groups with similar tasks for the purpose of checking work. Further, his students are highly motivated by his humor, reading level match, and the chance to help a peer do better with writing.

Grade 2 Language Arts: Alphabetizing

Ms. Howe has built several alphabetizing boards with the heads of large nails protruding from brightly colored plywood. Students practice their alphabetizing skills by hanging words on the nails in appropriate order.

Ms. Howe gives a student a cup of round, paper key tags with metal rims. Each tag has a word to be alphabetized. Some cups contain unfamiliar words with few syllables and distinctly different initial letters. Others contain words that closely resemble one another in spelling or configuration. Sometimes she puts a made-up word on a tag, and students are rewarded if they spot the phony word and can "prove" to the class why it's fake (by citing a rule or using a dictionary entry as evidence).

Differentiating what? The activity, or process, stays essentially the same. It's the material, or content, that varies.

Differentiating how? Again, skill readiness is the focus of differentiation. For one student, ordering words like *car* and *cap* presents a considerable challenge. For another, words like *choose* and *chose* or *library* and *librarian* are more appropriately challenging.

Differentiating why? Here, too, efficiency of learning and access to understanding are important to the teacher. Ms. Howe tries to meet students where their skills currently are, and she wants to help each child move on as rapidly as possible. It's important to remember that one set of materials may have a long life-span. A cup of tags that challenges a grade-level reader in September may be just right in December for a student whose skills are developing more slowly.

Grade 8 Physical Education: Volleyball Skills

Mr. Grant often organizes whole-class volleyball games in his physical education classes so his students can learn to function as a team. At other times, he divides the class in half. At one end of the gym, students play a volleyball game. Mr. Grant asks different students to referee these games: students with leadership skills and students who are comfortable with the sport. At the other end of the gym, he assembles a group of students who need to perfect a common skill, such as setting the ball, spiking the ball, or receiving the ball without shrinking from it. Students in the groups for direct instruction vary often and widely.

Differentiating what? Mr. Grant is differentiating the opportunity students have to develop mastery of specific skills. Both the particular skill (content) and the small-group activity (process) vary.

Differentiating how? In large measure, he is focusing on student readiness in a skill. He also may be attending to student learning profile when he gives students with leadership strength an opportunity to hone those skills.

Differentiating why? Students feel better about their participation in a sport when they can develop their prowess in it (motivation). They have greater access to that opportunity when their individual needs are addressed in a systematic, focused way for at least some of the class time.

High School Biology: Vocabulary Development

Ms. Cunard's biology classes include a number of students who are learning English as they also work to master the content of biology. She often "front-loads" vocabulary with these students prior to the beginning of a chapter or unit of study. In many instances, she finds it helpful to include in the front-loading discussions students whose text comprehension is weak, students with learning disabilities for whom complex vocabulary is a challenge, and other students who struggle with vocabulary for a variety of reasons.

Sometime before beginning a unit, Ms. Cunard meets for about 15 or 20 minutes with the students who are likely to benefit from front-loading. Other students work individually or in small groups on teacher-assigned tasks related to their current unit of study.

She presents to the smaller group six to eight vocabulary words that will be critical to their understanding of the upcoming unit. To help students unlock meaning in the words, she asks questions; provides examples, using familiar words that sound like the new vocabulary; highlights context clues; or helps them learn to use root words. The goal of the small-group work is to develop definitions that are clearly and succinctly written in words that are accessible to the students. Ms. Cunard will put the words on a "key word" bulletin board and will refer to them often through the unit.

Differentiating what? Ms. Cunard is differentiating both content and process. Content differentiation is not in the material itself but in the timing of the material's introduction. She is differentiating process in providing scaffolding for students who need it, while enabling students who can master the vocabulary more independently to do so.

Differentiating how? Front-loading is generally differentiation based on readiness. In some cases, however, Ms. Cunard includes in front-loading discussions students who learn best when in small groups (where focus is easier for them to maintain) or students who learn much more readily aurally than through reading.

Differentiating why? Ms. Cunard does not front-load vocabulary with the whole class; some students already know the words, and others can learn them from text and class discussions—goals she has for all her students. Her goal is to move all her students forward in both knowledge and learning skills, not to have some of them march in place or move backward. Front-loading key vocabulary enables her to provide scaffolding for students who need it at a given time without creating "backward momentum" for others.

High School World Languages: Understanding Grammatical Patterns

A pattern-focused exercise for Mrs. Higgins's German I class emphasizes formation and use of past-tense verbs. But Mrs. Higgins's students vary quite widely in speed and facility with learning a foreign language.

One group of students having difficulty with grammatical concepts in general, and German in particular, will work with pattern exercises in which much of a German sentence is supplied. However, each sentence uses an English verb, and students must supply the correct form of the past-tense German verb. Occasionally, an English noun or pronoun also appears, and students must supply the correct German verb. Mrs. Higgins has ensured that the missing verbs are regular and that other missing elements are essential to basic translation and conversation.

A second, somewhat more proficient group has a similar activity. But they will encounter a greater number and complexity of missing words, including a few irregular verbs. A third group of students works with the same sentences as the second group, but virtually all of the sentences are in English and must be translated into German. Two or three students in Mrs. Higgins's classes don't need the skill exercises because formative assessment and class observations indicate these students have already mastered these forms. She gives these students a scenario to develop, with instructions about the sorts of grammatical constructions that must be included. They may develop the scenario for written or taped presentation. A task that one group completes today may become homework for a less advanced group within the next few days.

Differentiating what? Students are practicing with varied content. Although all the students focus on past-tense verbs, their assignments vary other sentence and vocabulary elements.

Differentiating how? Student readiness is targeted, based on proficiency in providing basic grammatical constructions.

Differentiating why? Some of Mrs. Higgins's students need an additional, guided chance to practice basic, regular verb formation before moving on to other challenges. Other students are ready to grapple with the more complex and unpredictable irregular verbs; they can draw on a greater range of sentence elements and vocabulary. When she varies requirements by degrees of complexity, independence, and open-endedness, Mrs. Higgins ensures that all students escalate smoothly in skill from their current comfort levels. Having students work with readiness-appropriate tasks also enables her to better target direct instruction and monitor small groups. This process, which she uses every few days, ensures that students struggling with German don't add to their confusion and sense of failure by skipping steps of understanding. It also ensures that quick learners don't "stand still" and develop a sense of complacency with the language. It enables all students to work more competently and confidently with oral and written application tasks that are central in the class.

Grade 6 Language Arts: Spelling

Ms. Estes pre-tests her students on spelling in September. Typically, she identifies both students who work with 2nd grade words and those who top out on an 8th grade list, as well as the range in between. She uses a spelling procedure that is the same for all students, but each student works on a particular list indicated by current spelling performance. She color-codes the lists rather than labeling them with grade equivalents.

Students have a spelling notebook in which they write 10 words from their spelling list. Students create sentences with their words; have a peer check them; correct errors; take them to Ms. Estes for a final check; correct any remaining errors; write each word five times; and then take a quiz on the 10 words, which is administered by a peer. Any words missed become part of their next list. Ms. Estes gives individual survey tests on numerous past lists on a rotating basis. Again, misspelled words are "recycled" onto the next list.

The repetitions in this procedure prove to be quite effective in helping students internalize key spelling patterns. Students who demonstrate proficiency with 8th grade words at any point in the year work with a vocabulary procedure that emphasizes root words and derivatives from a variety of languages that have contributed to the evolution of English. In two of her classes, there are students for whom Ms. Estes is currently their primary spelling partner. They sit in an area of the classroom she often uses for student conferences so she can get to them easily. She checks in with them often and provides goals for work completion. These students may have individualized education plans that specify specific language goals; others are students who have difficulty collaborating with peers. When appropriate, she likes to have students check each other's work, but when that seems ill advised, she checks the work herself. As the year progresses and students become more comfortable with classroom routines, Ms. Estes will modify these students' work plans to allow interaction with a larger number of classmates.

Differentiating what? Ms. Estes is differentiating content by varying the spelling lists. The process or activity remains the same for all students, except for those who have tested out of spelling. For them, both content and process are modified. She is also modifying learning environment (seating arrangements) and affect (teacher-provided structure to support safety and achievement) for students who are not currently ready to work independently in the class at large.

Differentiating how? All of the spelling differentiation is based on ongoing assessment of student readiness.

Differentiating why? This procedure provides access to growth for all students at a rate appropriate for them individually. Independence and peer assistance are both quite motivating to the middle schoolers.

Grade 7 (All Subjects): Reviewing to Cement Facts and Skills

Blitzball is a big hit on the 7th grade team. A number of teachers use it to review ideas and information and to help students latch onto important knowledge and understandings.

Using teacher review guides, students work in mixed-readiness groups of four to six to make sure they know and understand key information. Then the teams compete in Blitzball: the teacher calls on a student, who comes to a line made of masking tape. The teacher asks the student a question. When the student answers correctly, he earns a chance to throw a tennis ball at a brightly painted plywood backboard with four small holes at each corner and a large hole in the center. Hitting the board gets one point for the team, sending the ball through the center hole nets three points, and a team earns five points when the ball goes through one of the small holes.

Students in the audience who talk during the game lose five points for their team. All the students stay alert for toss-up questions and opportunities to challenge answers for points. Teachers adjust questions based on students' level of understanding and skill to ensure that all students are appropriately challenged and have a fair chance to earn team points.

Differentiating what? Content is differentiated; the activity or process remains constant.

Differentiating how? The teacher differentiates by student readiness in the particular content at a particular time.

Differentiating why? Students are highly motivated by the fast-paced game, and they are even more motivated because everyone has an equal chance of earning a toss. An interesting additional motivator stems from the reality that capacity to throw a ball skillfully does not necessarily correlate with student readiness in a subject; maximum points are often earned by students who may not be academic stars.

Other Principles Reflected in the Examples

Skills-based activities are not always high on the engagement scale. But many teachers have been effective in making their activities user-friendly with humor, opportunities for movement, and student collaboration. In all of these instances, the activities are equally respectful in that one version doesn't look preferable to or less desirable than another. Although every student is squarely focused on the skill the teacher deems essential to practice, the activity in which the practice occurs is designed to be appealing for everyone.

These examples also illustrate teachers using ongoing assessment of student readiness, interest, and learning profile for the purpose of matching task to student need. They do not force-fit students to tasks. Readiness relates to a particular competency at a particular time; it does not equate to a statement about a child's overall capacity as a learner. Tasks change often and students are not grouped or seen as "slow learners" or "smart kids."

A child who is a very apt thinker in literature may have difficulty spelling. A student who spells well may have difficulty with reading comprehension. A child who has a beastly time writing German sentences may do quite well with oral language. Some students struggle with many things, and others are advanced with many things, but most have areas in which they are more fluid and others in which they are less fluid. It is fairer and more accurate to look at readiness for a specific skill at a given time instead of using one skill to make a judgment about general ability.

Teachers in these illustrations are crafting escalators of learning. They do not assume there is one spelling list for all 6th graders, one set of volleyball skills for all 7th graders, or one set of sentences for every novice German student. These teachers demonstrate a systematic intent to find students who are one floor—or two or three—below performance expectations and to move them up with minimal gaps and no sense of despair. There is also systematic intent to find learners who are a floor—or two or three—above performance expectations and to move them further upward with minimal "marching in place" and a sense that learning is synonymous with striving and challenge.

Differentiating Concept- or Meaning-Based Instruction

The principles and beliefs reflected in the previous section are still at work in the examples of differentiated instruction that follow. However, the next examples demonstrate a teacher's intent to integrate several or all levels of learning—facts, concepts, principles, attitudes, and skills. These teachers also differentiate curriculum and instruction from that very rich starting point, which focuses all students on making meaning of (or understanding) what they are learning.

Grade 12 Government: Evolution of Government and Societies

Over a period of three weeks, seniors in Mr. Yin's government class are conducting research in groups of three to five. Their goal is to understand how the Bill of Rights has expanded over time and its current impact on various groups in society. Continuing an ongoing exploration of the concept of change, they will explore the principle that the documents and institutions that govern societies change to meet the demands of changing times. The project requires them to work with skills of research and expository writing.

Mr. Yin has placed students in "investigation groups" of somewhat similar reading readiness (e.g., struggling readers to grade-level readers, grade-level readers to advanced readers). All research groups will work on and off over three weeks as the unit progresses, examining issues such as

• How one or more amendments in the Bill of Rights became more inclusive over time;

• Societal events that prompted reinterpretation of one or more amendments in the Bill of Rights;

• Court decisions that redefined one or more of the amendments;

• Current interpretations and applications of one or more of the amendments; and

• Unresolved issues related to the amendments.

Mr. Yin's students have a common rubric for the structure and content of appropriate writing, and every student will develop a written piece that stems from what they learn from their group's research. A wide range of print, Internet, video, and audio resources is available to all groups.

Despite common elements in the assignment, Mr. Yin has differentiated the work in two important ways. Some groups will research societal groups that are familiar to them, areas where issues are more clearly defined, or areas where there is more information available on a basic reading level. Other groups will examine unfamiliar societal groups, issues that are less defined, or issues where resources are more complex.

Students may choose to write an essay, parody, or dialogue to reflect their understandings. They may also propose another format. Mr. Yin provides brief guidelines for each form as well as a rubric that specifies expectations across forms.

Differentiating what? Although questions in the activity remain constant, the lenses through which students investigate those questions vary. In that way, the teacher has differentiated process. The culminating product offers variety in mode of expression. Content varies in that students will use a range of resources at varied levels of reading complexity.

Differentiating how? Mr. Yin has modified instruction based on students' sophistication in reading, writing, and abstract thinking. (He could have modified for interest as well, by encouraging students to select a societal group in which they were particularly interested.) The three product options address both readiness and learning profile. The essay is likely to require less complex thought and manipulation of language than the parody. Some students might be more drawn to the dialogue format than to the essay format. Although the option for students to propose an alternative format allows them to work with video, web-based presentations, annotated art forms, and so on, the criteria for required content and skills remain constant across formats.

Differentiating why? Mr. Yin sees access to materials as an important issue. Research materials and sources differ greatly in complexity, and issues can differ greatly in clarity. By matching students to materials and issues, he maximizes the likelihood that students will come away appropriately challenged. They also will have a grasp of essential concepts and principles. Similarly, he has provided product options at varying degrees of difficulty. Making some choices for the product himself and encouraging students to make others balances Mr. Yin's role as diagnostician with students' needs to make decisions about their own learning.

Grade 1 (All Subjects): Patterns

Mr. Morgan and his 1st graders look for patterns in language, art, music, science, and numbers—everywhere they go and in everything they study. They understand the principles that patterns use repetition and that patterns are predictable. Today, Mr. Morgan and his students are working with patterns in writing.

As a whole class, they have looked at how writers like Dr. Seuss use language patterns. They've clapped out the patterns together; recited them; and talked about sounds, words, and sentences. They have listened to their teacher read part of a pattern in a book, and they have predicted what might come next.

Mr. Morgan just read his students *The Important Book* by Margaret Wise Brown (1949), which also uses patterns. The pattern it uses is "The important thing about _____ is that it is _____. It is _____. It is _____. And it is _____. But the important thing about _____ is that it is _____." (For example: "The important thing about night is that it is dark. It is quiet. It is creepy. And it is scary. But the important thing about night is that it is dark.")

Now the 1st graders are going to make an Important Book for their class, showing how they can use writing patterns. Mr. Morgan will have them work in groups to develop the pages. Some students who need more assistance with the concept of a pattern and with writing itself will work with him to select the important object they will write about. He will guide them as they tell him what to write on chart paper, making sure they work together to select a topic, describe what's important about it, and complete the pattern. He also will have them take turns reading their page, individually and as a group, and he will have each student talk about the repetition in the pattern and how it is predictable. Once the chart page is completed, Mr. Morgan will convert it into a book-sized page that matches others being created in the class.

Some students will work in pairs to complete a template that Mr. Morgan has created. They will select their own language to complete the template and do the writing themselves. However, Mr. Morgan has given these students a list of nouns and adjectives from which they can draw if they "get stuck." A few students in the class are very advanced with writing. Their job is to create a page for the book "from scratch." They may refer to the original book if they need to, but most will develop the page from memory and can manage the writing adequately on their own. Mr. Morgan has provided these students with challenging criteria for their work, and they will submit drafts of their work to peers and to him for suggestions on enhancing the quality of their initial drafts.

Mr. Morgan will ask students from all working groups to read their pages to the class at some time over the next few days. He'll use this opportunity to have students talk about what a pattern is and how patterns are used in their book. Students will work together in heterogeneous reading groups to illustrate the book pages, make a cover and title page (both of which are examples of patterns in books), bind the book, and add it to a growing collection of books about patterns they have created for their class library.

Differentiating what? Content in this scenario stays basically the same; all students are working with the same concept and principles, and all are working with skills of writing. The process varies, as Mr. Morgan provides varied levels and kinds of support and guidance in making the book pages.

Differentiating how? Based on his assessment of student proficiency in writing and in developing patterns in writing, Mr. Morgan differentiates the activity in response to student readiness.

Differentiating why? In most 1st grade classes, students demonstrate a wide range of language skills. In this case, all students need a chance to explore patterns, recognize patterns, contribute to pattern formation, work with writing skills, and contribute to the work of the class. However, to be appropriately challenging for the full span of language development, the writing task needs to be provided at varying degrees of structure and with varied degrees of support in order to respond to varied stages of language development.

Grade 9 U.S. History: Revolution and Change

Mrs. Lupold and her 9th graders are studying the Industrial Revolution in the United States. She has developed a concept-based unit that attends to student commonalities as well as their differences in readiness, interest, and learning profile. This unit (and others throughout the year) is based on ideas such as interdependence, change, revolution, and scarcity versus plenty. Students will examine principles such as

- Changes in one part of a society affect other parts of the society;
- People resist change;
- Change is necessary for progress;
- When members of a society have uneven access to economic resources, conflict often arises; and

• The struggles of one historical period are much like those of other historical periods.

Among the skills emphasized are comprehension of text materials, note taking, analysis, and identification and transfer of historical themes. Knowledge includes key events of the Industrial Revolution, causes and effects of the time period, and vocabulary related to the time period.

Without telling students the name of the "new" time period they are about to study, Mrs. Lupold asks students to work with classmates at their assigned tables (random seating) to create a web or mind map of what was going on in history as their previous unit concluded. This helps them use what they already have learned to build a foundation for what is to come.

She invites students who like to read aloud to volunteer to take home excerpts from two novels. They can practice reading aloud so they will be prepared to read for the class the next day. She offers students who have difficulty reading selections from *Lyddie* by Katherine Paterson (1991), which are manageable by most students with below-grade reading skills. She offers stronger readers passages from *The Dollmaker* by Harriett Arnow (1954), a book for adult-level readers.

The next day, the student volunteers read powerful passages from the two novels describing living conditions during the Industrial Revolution in the United States (although the term itself isn't used). Using the think-pair-share-square strategy, Mrs. Lupold presents the pivotal question to the class: "What could possibly be going on in our country to have people living this way?" Students individually write about their ideas for two minutes, then turn to a thinking partner of their choice (someone close, so no walking is involved). They discuss their thoughts for two minutes, and then each pair is joined by another pair for a four-way exchange. After discussing the question for two more minutes, Mrs. Lupold poses the question again for whole-class discussion.

Eventually, she helps students link what they heard in the novels with the webs they drew the day before. She tells them the new period is called the Industrial Revolution, and she helps them speculate how that name predicts what will happen in the novels. They end class by creating a chart listing the things students know about the Industrial Revolution, things they think they know but aren't sure of, and things they want to know as their study progresses.

The next day, students watch a video about the time period and then select one of four journal prompts to complete in their learning logs. The prompts, all dealing with change, are at varying degrees of difficulty, but students are free to write on whichever prompt they choose. They then read their textbook and take notes on their reading using one of three organizers distributed by the teacher. The amount of structure in the organizers varies, and they are distributed based on Mrs. Lupold's ongoing assessment of students' skill with reading text materials.

As students read, Mrs. Lupold calls small groups to sit with her on the floor in the front of the room. She works with them on key vocabulary, interpretation of key passages, and direct reading, again based on her awareness of their needs as readers. When students complete reading a chapter, she gives them a quick formative assessment. At this point, the assessment is not for a grade but to better understand how to assign students to a key activity she is planning for the next couple of days.

Throughout the year, Mrs. Lupold works with students to identify and transfer key themes of history, guiding them to understand that people in one period have experiences much like those in others. As part of the current unit, Mrs. Lupold's class explores Paul Fleischman's *Dateline: Troy* (1996), which matches passages from *The Iliad* with clippings from modern newspapers and magazines to demonstrate how closely the events of today parallel those of the ancients. Although Fleischman's book deals with a period other than the Industrial Revolution, it reinforces the idea that the struggles of one period are much like those of another; this concept is the basis for the small-group activity that follows.

Based on student knowledge and understanding of essential information in the unit to this point—and based on her awareness of their proficiency in reading and thinking about history—Mrs. Lupold assigns students to one of four groups (Groups T, R, O, and Y). Each group will identify key themes in the Industrial Revolution and compare the themes to current events. The activity for each group is slightly different, designed to match students' level of readiness.

Group T's activity will imitate Fleischman's *Dateline: Troy*. Their instructions, which include examples of "important things," read as follows:

> The author shows us that a lottery was used to determine who joined the army 3,000 years ago and in the Vietnam War. Now, work in pairs and take

a second look at the video on the Industrial Revolution. Use it and the textbook to find important things that happened during that time. Check your list of key themes with me before going ahead with the rest of the assignment. What you'll do then is watch TV news programs and find current events similar to what was happening in the Industrial Revolution.

Group T students use a three-column grid provided by Mrs. Lupold to list a key event in the Industrial Revolution, a current event, and how the two are alike. As a culminating project, they will show their classmates a news clip and explain how the event in it is like an event in the Industrial Revolution. Mrs. Lupold encourages them to develop a visual of their grid (for the overhead or as a large poster) or make a graphic organizer to use during the explanation. All students in the group need to be ready to present information.

The instructions for Group R first have them connect the right- and left-hand pages in *Dateline: Troy*. (For example, "What is the problem shared by Achilles on page 48 and Darryl Strawberry on page 49?") Next, they think about key events in the Industrial Revolution and search sources such as *Time*, *Scholastic News*, *Newsweek*, and online newspapers to find five possible matches. They will select their two best matches, defending to the teacher why the two are "best" before they continue. Ultimately, they will create two parallel pages for a book called *Dateline: Industrial Revolution*, which will list events from the Industrial Revolution on the left-hand pages and collages of articles from "matching" news sources on the right. Students can use cartoons, computer graphics, headlines, and drawings along with the news articles themselves. All students in the group have to be ready to present, explain, and defend the pages to classmates.

Students in Group O also look at *Dateline: Troy* with the intention of creating a parallel book excerpt for the Industrial Revolution. They will select eight or so events from the Industrial Revolution that demonstrate the revolutionary nature of the time. Then, they will identify parallel "revolutions" in this century, create or find collage materials that make the parallels clear, and devise a way to both tell and show the parallel nature of the two revolutions in their own book. Students have to clear their plans for the book segment with Mrs. Lupold before executing them. They will focus on using insightful language and visuals, and all members of the group have to be prepared to share and interpret their creation.

Group Y students' instructions are as follows:

> The period we are studying is called the Industrial Revolution, yet there was no army or fighting as in the French Revolution, American Revolution, or Russian Revolution. It's also possible for individuals to have revolutionary experiences. Using *Dateline: Troy* as a model, develop a way to think about and show what you would consider to be essential elements in any revolution (such as rapid change, fear, or danger). Your comparison must include the Industrial Revolution, an individual revolution, and a military revolution. It must use important, valid, and defensible themes. It also must be effective in communicating your ideas: accurate, insightful, articulate, visually powerful, and easy to follow.

As the unit draws to a close, Mrs. Lupold presents a lecture on the Industrial Revolution to highlight information, ideas, and themes she wants to reinforce. She uses a learner-friendly format, planning the flow of her lecture, displaying a graphic organizer that follows the lecture sequence (to guide note taking), and delivering the lecture in segments of about five minutes. She follows each segment with a class discussion and summary of key points, a key question for students to consider, or a prediction for students to make based on what they are hearing and thinking.

Next, students in Groups T and R use their tiered activity materials to help her demonstrate how the Industrial Revolution isn't so different from today. Then the class continues to explore the idea through four-by-four sharing. Sharing groups combining students from each of the four tiered activity groups use their dateline materials to illustrate the following:

- How the Industrial Revolution relates to our lives;
- Key events in the Industrial Revolution;
- Key themes or elements in the Industrial Revolution; and
- How the Industrial Revolution was revolutionary.

Mrs. Lupold does not assign questions to particular students, but by virtue of the tiered activity, every student is prepared to answer at least one question.

Students then complete a paired review for a quiz on the unit, using a study guide that includes important vocabulary, events, and themes. Students can self-select partners for review. But the quiz is not the sole assessment of students' grasp of the unit. They have also just completed individual products they began about three-quarters of the way through the unit. The product assignment asked students to develop a way to show a revolution in a person's life, the last 50 years, culture, a subject or a hobby area, or the future.

Students' products illustrate how key concepts and themes (change, scarcity and plenty, interdependence, danger) were reflected in the revolution they explored. Students express their findings and understandings of parallels to the Industrial Revolution through research papers, models, creative writing, drama, music, and other formats. For this assignment, they could work alone or in groups of up to four. Mrs. Lupold provided rubrics to ensure that the products all focus on essential knowledge, understanding, and skill. She also encouraged students to add to the rubrics specific criteria for their products and to present their expanded version to her for approval.

Differentiating what? Throughout the unit, Mrs. Lupold differentiates content (e.g., using videos as well as text materials), process (e.g., the tiered activity based on *Dateline: Troy*), and product (e.g., the product assignment that allowed different expressions of key understandings).

Differentiating how? Mrs. Lupold differentiates her teaching in response to readiness by offering novels on two levels for volunteers to read aloud and varying the concreteness/abstractness and structure/openness in the tiered assignment. She differentiates for interest through options for product applications and modes of expression. She differentiates by learning profile by giving students choices of working conditions for the product and when she calls on varied learning strengths in the tiered activities.

This is a teacher who demonstrates many key principles of differentiation. All students undertake respectful activities that are interesting, focus on essential ideas and skills, and are likely to promote both challenge and success for students with varying needs. Students work in many different groupings: randomly at their tables, with thinking partners of their choice, with another thinking set, alone, with students of like readiness, and with students of mixed readiness. The groupings shift according to both teacher choice and student choice.

Differentiating why? Mrs. Lupold knows that if she supports struggling learners (by using videos to supplement text materials, breaking a lecture into accessible parts, providing a review guide, or building more structure into the tiered assignment), they will be able to move from a concrete look at the events of the Industrial Revolution to a more abstract application. She also makes certain that advanced learners are challenged by offering advanced reading materials at several points, providing a very abstract and multifaceted version of the tiered assignment, and allowing opportunities for advanced students to work with peers of similar readiness. Although the lesson focuses on skills in reading, writing, and interpretation at varying levels, the conceptual focus of the unit is meaning-rich for all students. All of Mrs. Lupold's efforts make the Industrial Revolution more meaningful and memorable.

•   •   •

In all the examples of differentiation described in this chapter, teachers were clear about the essential facts, skills, and understandings (concepts, principles) that framed their subjects. The teachers also continually sought information to help them understand each student's point of entry and progress and then attempted to match curriculum and instruction to each learner's readiness, interest, or mode of learning. They wanted to provide students the opportunity to learn coherently, at an appropriate level of challenge, and in an engaging way. Each teacher wanted to link the learner and the learning, an important goal that's sometimes uncommonly difficult to envision amid one-size-fits-all classrooms.

7

Instructional Strategies That Support Differentiation

Only teachers who utilize a variety of instructional models will be successful in maximizing the achievement of all students. . . . Teachers need to "play to" students' strengths and to mitigate students' learning weaknesses. This can be done only through the use of instructional variety.

Thomas J. Lasley and Thomas J. Matczynski,
Strategies for Teaching in a Diverse Society

There's nothing inherently good or bad about instructional strategies. They are, in essence, the "buckets" teachers can use to deliver content, process, or products. Yet some buckets are better suited than others to achieve a particular goal. The buckets can be used artfully or clumsily as part of well-conceived or poorly conceived lesson plans and delivery. In addition, virtually all buckets can be used in ways that ignore student learning differences, or they can become part of a larger system that appropriately responds to those differences. As Hattie (2009) reminds us, it's not a particular instructional method or script that will make a difference in student learning, it's getting more precise about how students are progressing in their learning and then using that information to personalize learning. It's about choosing the strategy that will work best for a given learner at a given time.

For example, it would be grossly inefficient to use the instructional strategy called group investigation to introduce 3rd graders to the concept of fractions. Similarly, it would be ineffective to ask high school students to develop a stance on the ethical issue of genetic engineering using the instructional strategy called concept attainment. It makes no sense to expect a student who is learning English to benefit from a compelling web demonstration that is presented in English. Consider the nest of strategies we describe as cooperative learning: they have often fallen short of expectations not because of a deficiency in the strategies themselves but because teachers apply them shallowly.

Expert teachers generally are comfortable with a wide range of instructional strategies, and they vary them skillfully with the nature of the learning task and learners' needs (Berliner, 1986; Stronge, 2002). When correctly used, many instructional strategies invite teachers to respond to students' differences in readiness, interest, or learning profile. Some instructional strategies last only a short time during a lesson and require little planning; others help teachers shape an entire way of life in the classroom and require extensive planning and ongoing reflection. Whereas some strategies emphasize organization or arrangement of students for learning, others focus predominantly on the nature of instruction itself.

There are many avenues to creating an instructionally responsive classroom. As you read about instructional strategies in this chapter and the next, observe how teachers use them to create classrooms where students have the opportunity to work at a comfortable pace, at an individually challenging degree of difficulty, in learning modes that match learning profiles, and with applications that are personally intriguing.

As in the previous chapter, the instructional strategies are described in actual classroom scenarios and then analyzed according to what the teacher is differentiating, how the teacher is differentiating, and why the teacher is differentiating.

Stations

Stations are different spots in the classroom where students work on various tasks simultaneously. They can be used with students of every age and in all subjects. They can be a frequent or occasional part of the learning process. They can be formal or informal. They can be distinguished by signs, symbols, or colors, or the teacher simply can ask groups of students to move to particular parts of the room. (A strategy that is both like and different from stations is centers, which are discussed and illustrated in Chapter 8.)

For the purposes of differentiated instruction, stations allow different students to work with different tasks. They invite flexible grouping because not all students need to go to all stations all the time. Not all students need to spend the same amount of time at each station, either. Further, even when all students do go to every station, assignments at each station can vary from day to day based on who will rotate there. Stations also lend themselves to a good balance of teacher choice and student choice. On some days, the teacher decides who will go to a particular station, what work they will do when they get there, and the working conditions that must prevail while they are there. On other days, students can make these decisions. On still other days, the teacher may set some of the parameters, but the student can choose the rest.

Grade 4 Math: Stations

At the beginning of the year, math assessments show that Ms. Minor's 4th graders are "all over the place" with computation of whole numbers. She has presented the children with a variety of tasks involving computation at varying degrees of sophistication and in varied contexts, which has helped her assess their starting points. She has discovered that these learners represent quite a range of readiness, from two or three years below grade expectations to an equal distance above grade level.

Some of her 4th graders still have difficulty with basic math facts and algorithms, or rules of computation in addition or subtraction. These students are really lost with multiplication beyond rote memory of multiplication tables. Other students have a good understanding of the algorithms of number computation for addition, subtraction, and multiplication; they just need opportunities to apply their understandings in varied situations. These students also are ready to begin a formal exploration of division. Still other students no longer find the three basic operations either interesting or challenging as presented by the grade-level math text. Many of these students have an "instinctive" understanding of division. Some of them have had formal teaching about it, or they have taught themselves how to divide.

Another consideration for Ms. Minor is that her students' attention spans vary. Some can lose themselves in math tasks for lengthy periods; others find

10 minutes of concentrated work a strain. Further, she has discovered that length of attention span is not always a function of competency.

To begin the year, Ms. Minor gradually introduces her students to five learning stations, which are really just areas of the room. Each day, students look at a pegboard with nails that represent the five stations in the room. Key tags with student names hang in the various sections of the pegboard to let students know where to begin math class.

Station 1 is The Teaching Station. Students in Station 1 have direct instruction with the teacher. They meet with her near the whiteboard, and she teaches them and guides their work on a topic in number computation. Often, she leaves students in this group to work at the whiteboard or in pairs on the floor. They solve problems or practice skills as she circulates among the other stations. Students at Station 1 record their work at the station by finding their name on a clipboard chart and checking the date and kind of computation on which they worked.

Station 2 is Proof Place. Students in Station 2 use manipulatives or drawn representations to work with number computation and to explain and defend their work. This station helps students understand why numbers and number computations work as they do. They are assigned to the station with a partner, but first they work alone with a computation or series of computations in a folder with their name on it. They time their individual work with a five-minute digital timer. Then the partners share the tasks they were working on, how they decided what operation to use, and why they think their answers are correct. They may "prove" their work with drawings, diagrams, or manipulatives. Their partner checks their understanding by asking them to use a second method for thinking about their answer. Proof Place has posted prompts for students, such as the following:

> Use estimation to show whether your answer is probably right. Show me a diagram or picture that proves your way of thinking about the problem is right. Use the checkers in this cup to show the way you worked the problem is right.

Ultimately, students can check their partner's work with a calculator to see if answers agree. When they're done, students complete an audit card and attach it to the paper, alongside their work. The audit card says

> Today [student's name] worked on problems using [name of computation] and proved the method by using [diagrams, objects]. My partner was [name].

> The method we used to check my work was [estimation, objects, drawings]. When we checked with the calculator, it said [I was right, I need to think about this some more].

Students date the cards and leave the work and cards in a box at the station. They also sign out of the station on a chart, writing the date, checking the kind of computation, and checking the method they used to show their thinking.

Station 3 is Practice Plaza. At this station, students develop comfort, accuracy, and speed in a particular kind of computation using teacher-generated tasks, computer programs, apps that offer game-based practice on a range of math skills, or a textbook. When necessary, they check their work using an answer key, calculator, or computer. Finally, they write a self-evaluation of their work, referring, if necessary, to sample language at the station. They leave their signed and dated work in the appropriate box at the station; computer-based work generates a report for the teacher. They also find their name on a chart at the station. It asks for the date, the kind of computation they practiced, the number of problems attempted, and the number correct.

Students in Station 4, The Shop, work with math applications. The Shop is run by a man named Mr. Fuddle, who always seems to need their help. Items in the shop vary from time to time, as do tasks on which students work. But students always work with some facet of running a store or shopping at a store, and they always help Mr. Fuddle, who has somehow gotten himself into another mess.

Sometimes at The Shop, students "buy" from online or paper catalogs. Sometimes they make decisions about what to sell in the store and how much to buy based on a specified budget. Sometimes they count inventory and group items, and sometimes they make change for a series of purchases. Changing objects, varying tasks, and the presence of poor old Mr. Fuddle make going to The Shop fun. The Shop makes math something that is useful in the everyday world. When leaving The Shop, students write notes or e-mails to Mr. Fuddle, dating them and describing what problem he has gotten himself into, what they did to solve it, and what he should do next time to avoid the problem. They leave their notes in Mr. Fuddle's mailbox at the station or mail them to him in care of their teacher's school e-mail account.

Station 5 is Project Place. Here students work alone, in pairs, or in small groups to complete long-term projects that require the use of mathematics in a variety of forms. The length of projects and the topics vary. Sometimes projects deal with classroom issues such as designing a center, redesigning the classroom, or conducting and reporting surveys about students. Sometimes they deal with sports, outer space, literature, or writing. Sometimes the teacher thinks of project ideas. Sometimes students do. What all projects have in common is that students use mathematics in a way that connects it to a larger world and in a way that piques student interest. Students keep project logs in which they make two entries whenever they are at Project Place. At the beginning of class, they summarize what they have done so far on their project, and they set goals for the day. At the end of class, they write about how they did with their goals and their next steps. Their project logs stay at the project center in a file box.

Some days, Ms. Minor teaches whole-class math lessons, conducts whole-class reviews, plays whole-class math games, or runs whole-class "contests." On those days, no student names are on the pegboard. Occasionally, one or two stations are "closed for the day." Most days, however, students are assigned to one of the five stations to work. All students go to all stations in the course of a week or 10 days. Not all students spend the same amount of time at each station in a given two-week period, and not all students rotate through the stations in the same order. Sometimes students work at a station with students of similar readiness, and sometimes they work with students of differing readiness.

Ms. Minor uses students' record-keeping forms, work, and planning logs along with periodic formal assessments to assign students to stations. One day, for example, she worked at The Teaching Station with six students to review multiplication of two-digit numbers. Two of those students stayed at the station for a second day, and she added two students who had been working fairly well with two-digit multiplication but had been sick and absent for several days. Of the four students who left The Teaching Station, two went to Proof Place (along with several other pairs of students who were working on a variety of computations). Two others went to Practice Plaza to hone their computation of two-digit numbers. At Project Place, eight students worked on three different long-term projects. In each of the three groups, some members were at other stations that day. Students understand that often group members will work in other places. Project logs help all members of a group keep up with one another's progress on the joint effort.

Ms. Minor is keenly aware of the content standards that her students are expected to reach, and she always plans with those in mind. When students are lagging behind with math proficiency, she works with them on knowledge, skills, and understanding targeted at closing the gaps that make it impossible for them to move ahead. At the same time, she plans tasks, homework, and direct instruction sessions to introduce students to the content that typically comes next in the learning sequence. When students demonstrate advanced math proficiency, she plans tasks, homework, and direct instruction that extend student understanding, increase the challenge level, or introduce content that typically comes next in the learning sequence.

Differentiating what? Ms. Minor differentiates both content and process at The Teaching Station, Proof Place, Practice Plaza, and The Shop. All students work with math reasoning, math application, and math practice; the particular operations, their degree of difficulty, and the degree of difficulty of activities are varied to provide a good fit for students based on Ms. Minor's ongoing assessment of their strengths and needs. She also differentiates products at Project Place. These vary in complexity, duration, group composition, skills required, and other variables, based on her continual assessment of learners' needs.

Differentiating how? Ms. Minor differentiates predominantly by student readiness at Stations 1 through 4, with students of similar readiness working on tasks at a similar difficulty level. Station 5 often, but not always, involves students of varying readiness working on projects together. Station 4 (The Shop) addresses interest by varying materials and problems based on the different materials. Station 5 (Project Place) always places a strong emphasis on student interest. It offers a wide range of project options and modes of expression. The various ways to think about and demonstrate math reasoning in Proof Place address her students' different learning profile needs and the fact that they will grasp math through different approaches.

Differentiating why? Essential understandings and skills about math operations are more accessible to students when presented at their readiness levels. Motivation is high because of the variety of approaches to learning math, varied materials and product options, and the opportunity to work with a variety of students. Targeted use of stations makes both teaching and learning more efficient than it could be with whole-class instruction or if all students spent the same amount of time at each station and completed the same work at each station.

Other considerations. Ms. Minor uses stations in a way that accentuates the concept of flexible grouping. Even in The Teaching Place, where students receive similar direct instruction, they stay for different amounts of time. At Stations 2 through 4, students of varied readiness levels may work at the same station but on different tasks. Also, because rotation does not progress in a certain order, and because the length of assignment to a center varies with student need, students have a sense that "everyone does a bunch of different things" in their math class. They have no sense of specific, ability-based math groups. An additional layer of ambiguity about why students work in a given spot at a given time is added as the teacher sometimes assigns students to The Shop based on interest (for example, sending students who like sports to The Shop on a day when materials and tasks revolve around ordering, inventorying, or purchasing athletic materials) and by student choice in math application projects at Project Place.

Agendas

An agenda is a personalized list of tasks that a particular student must complete in a specified time (see Figure 7.1). Student agendas throughout a course will have similar and dissimilar elements. A teacher usually creates an agenda that will last a student two to three weeks, but the duration can vary. The teacher develops a new agenda when the previous one is completed.

Generally, students determine the order in which they will complete agenda items. A particular time in the day is set aside as "agenda time." In elementary classrooms and block-scheduled secondary classrooms, teachers often select the first part of the day or block. In other classes, agendas are used once a week or as anchor activities when students complete other assigned work.

While students work on their agendas, the teacher has great freedom to move among individual students, coaching and monitoring their understanding and progress. The teacher also can take advantage of agenda time to assemble small groups of students who need guided work or direct instruction with a particular concept or skill. Agendas can also be used for homework rather than classwork, for both classwork and homework, or for an anchor activity when students complete assigned classwork.

Figure 7.1 A Personal Agenda

Teacher and Student Initials at Successful Completion	Task	Special Instructions
	Complete a computer animation showing how a volcano works.	Be sure to show scientific accuracy in your explanation of the animation.
	Read your personal-choice biography.	Keep a reading log of your progress.
	Practice adding fractions by completing the green assignment at the computer station.	Come to the teacher or a classmate for help if you get stuck.
	Complete research for an article on why volcanoes are where they are for our science newsletter. Write the article. Have the editor review it with you. Revise as needed.	Watch your punctuation and spelling! Don't let them affect your great skill at organizing ideas.
	Compete at least two spelling cycles.	

Grade 5 (Various Subjects): Agendas

As students enter their classroom each morning, they put away their jackets and books, say hello to classmates and their teacher, Ms. Clayter, and go to the box that holds their agenda folders. After morning announcements, each student completes a daily planning log, which contains the student's goals for completing the day's agenda tasks. Students who know they need teacher assistance can write a request for a conference on the board above the agenda box. Students then move to various parts of the room to begin working on their tasks.

Many students work alone with reading, writing, math, or independent investigations. In several places in the room, students cluster in twos or threes, often on carpet squares, to complete collaborative tasks.

After Ms. Clayter circulates to make certain everyone begins work in a focused and orderly manner, she calls three boys to sit with her on the floor near the bookshelves. For the next several minutes, she discusses the computer animation of a volcano they completed the day before. She tells the boys she thought their graphics were really impressive. They agree. She then asks them to review the written goals for the task. Among those is the goal that anyone who views the animation will come away with a clear understanding of what makes a volcano erupt. With her guidance, the boys admit that their labels and annotation for the animation fell short of this goal. She leaves them to write a plan, which they must present to her, to ensure their work meets all objectives.

Ms. Clayter then moves to a pair of students coauthoring poems. She has paired the two students to work with poetry as part of their agendas because each has something important to teach the other. Jenna is highly imaginative and uses language like a paintbrush to make images for her readers, but she lacks persistence when it comes to polishing her work. Han is less fluent with her imagery, in part because English is her second language. She moved to the United States in 2nd grade. On the other hand, Han's love of poetry is electric, and her work ethic is immense. The two girls enjoy working together, and Ms. Clayter knows they can strengthen each other's writing. She asks them to read aloud their latest piece of writing, tells them several things she finds effective in the poem, and leaves them with two challenges to think about as they work for the remainder of agenda time.

Two boys who need additional practice with math are working on a mystery that asks them to select and use appropriate operations to solve a math problem. The math required is at a relatively basic level, but the mystery format is inviting. The boys keep a record of mysteries they solve to get "promotions points" that will earn them certificates and badges as math detectives.

As Ms. Clayter creates student agendas, she has four goals: developing student work that focuses on essential learning outcomes in one or more core content areas, building on strengths, shoring up deficits, and fostering independence. Thus, each student's agenda includes work in each of these areas. In a two- to three-week agenda cycle, all students are likely to work in several subject areas—in each instance with practice, application, or transfer of essential knowledge, understanding, or skills. They'll work with some things they love and some they could do without. All students will set and monitor daily and weekly goals. All will work alone and with peers. All will meet with the teacher informally and formally throughout the agenda period, both at the teacher's request and at their own.

Ms. Clayter finds agendas a great way to attend to student differences in readiness, interest, and learning profile. At this one time in the day, she can extend and support student growth in all subject areas. Her students love the calm way to ease into the school day, the variety, and the sense of autonomy the agendas provide.

Differentiating what? Using student agendas allows Ms. Clayter to differentiate virtually anything. She can differentiate content by varying materials, subjects, topics within subjects, and degree of teacher support. She can differentiate process or sense making by varying the degree of difficulty of tasks as well as ways students make sense of ideas. Agendas also allow for pacing variation. Students can have differing amounts of time to make sense of a particular skill or concept. Agendas also facilitate product differentiation by providing time for students to work on long-term products in class where the teacher can monitor and coach their planning, research, quality of thought, and production.

Differentiating how? Agendas allow great flexibility for modifications based on student readiness, interest, and learning profile. Ms. Clayter can form like-readiness or mixed-readiness groups. She can form groups of students whose skills in a particular area lag, or she can form groups with students who have long since mastered basic expectations. She can point individual students toward materials and tasks they will find appropriately challenging. She can vary working conditions and modes through which students can explore and express learning. Students may work either independently or collaboratively. Agendas also enable her to tap into student interests. Agenda time provides a tailor-made chance to have one student work with fractions through music, another with fractions through baseball trading cards, and still another with fractions through stock market reports.

Differentiating why? Ms. Clayter is a relatively new teacher. Her students have shown her a wide range of interests and needs in all subjects, and figuring out how to modify curriculum and instruction in every subject all day long is a bit of a challenge for her. Using agendas allows Ms. Clayter to concentrate her efforts at differentiation during one time of the day and still be effective in addressing a great array of student needs. She finds she can achieve most of the goals of differentiation through agendas, and she does so in a way that makes her planning more manageable at this point in her career than if she tried to differentiate lessons in multiple subjects throughout the day.

Complex Instruction

Complex instruction is a strategy that responds to the sorts of academic ranges that frequently exist in classrooms that are academically, culturally, and linguistically heterogeneous (Cohen, 1994; Watanabe, 2012). Its goal is to establish equity of learning opportunity for all students in the context of intellectually challenging materials and through the use of small instructional groups. Like most promising classroom approaches, complex instruction is itself complex, and it requires considerable reflection and planning. The payoff, however, can be immense. It helps establish a classroom in which the contributions of every individual are prized by all, and high-level instruction is standard fare for all learners.

Complex instruction tasks

- Require students to work together in small, heterogeneous groups;
- Are designed to draw upon the intellectual strengths of each student in the group;
- Are open-ended;
- Are intrinsically interesting to students;
- Allow for a variety of solutions and solution routes;
- Involve real objects;
- Provide materials and instructions in multiple languages (if students in the class represent varied language groups);
- Integrate reading and writing in ways that make them an important means to accomplishing a desirable goal;
- Draw upon multiple abilities in a real-world way;
- Use multimedia; and
- Require many different talents in order to be completed adequately.

An effective complex instruction task *does not*

- Have a single right answer;
- Allow for completion more efficiently by one or two students than by the whole group;
- Reflect low-level thinking; or
- Involve simple memorization of routine learning.

Teachers who use complex instruction move among groups as they work, asking students questions about the work, probing their thinking, and facilitating understanding. Over time, teachers also delegate increasing authority for learning to students. They then support students in developing the skills needed to manage the authority well.

Two additional—and vital—teacher roles are discovering students' intellectual strengths and "assignment of status." Cohen (1994) reflects that traditional cooperative groups often fail because students know who is "good at school" and who is not. Those who are good are given (or take) responsibility for successful completion of group tasks. Those who are not "good at school" relinquish (or have taken from them) responsibility for successful completion of academic tasks. This, says Cohen, stems from the fact that many school tasks are highly dependent on encoding, decoding, computation, and memorization. Those things become synonymous with school success in the minds of students as well as teachers.

Complex instruction seeks tasks that call on a much wider range of intellectual skills, such as generating ideas, asking probing questions, representing ideas symbolically, using rhythm to interpret or express ideas, hypothesizing, and planning. Teachers study students continually and systematically to identify individual strengths, then design complex instruction tasks that call upon various student abilities.

In "assignment of status," teachers seek key moments in group work when a student (often one not perceived as "successful" by peers) makes a worthwhile comment or suggestion. The teacher articulates to the group what he heard the student say and why he feels it is a contribution to the work of the whole group. Students begin to see peers in a different light, and they also begin to develop a vocabulary that reflects a wide range of intellectual strengths. Finally, in presenting complex instruction tasks to the class, the teacher leads the students in listing the full range of intellectual tasks required for successful completion of the work. This helps them understand that all students have some of the required strengths but no one has all of them.

Grade 10 English: Complex Instruction

In Ms. McCleary's 10th grade English classes, students have been studying how writers' lives and works intertwine. They have read a variety of types of literature this year, including poetry, and they've looked at writing as "mirror and metaphor." That is, they have explored how a piece of writing can become a metaphor for a larger idea, and they have explored how writing holds a mirror up to readers to allow them to better understand themselves and their world. Students recently completed a "stepping stones" writing assignment in which they diagrammed and wrote about the events in their own lives that were most important in shaping them.

Today, Ms. McCleary's students will begin work on a complex instruction task. They will work in small groups for the next four or five class periods to complete the task, sharing what they have learned with the whole group during an additional class period. Homework during this time also focuses on the group's tasks. The task will be one key element of student assessment when the marking period ends. Ms. McCleary has given each group a task card (see Figure 7.2).

Differentiating what? Ms. McCleary uses the complex instruction task to differentiate content by providing books of varying reading levels and in varied languages along with videos, music, and other resources. She does this while ensuring all students focus on the same essential understandings. She differentiates process by providing multiple segments of a rich task that allow students to make sense of ideas in a range of ways. Here, the 20-minute presentation (product) is differentiated in that students will "specialize" in one facet of the larger project.

Differentiating how? Ms. McCleary's use of complex instruction provides for readiness differentiation through varied kinds and sources of materials, interest differentiation in selection of biographical subjects, and learning profile differentiation with investigation and expression through multiple modes of intelligence. She offers resource materials and instructions in multiple languages when possible so that students new to English will be able to help others access success. When possible, she ensures that students new to English are in groups with another student who speaks both that student's first language and English and can serve as a bridge between languages so the student who is learning English is not left out of the deliberations and work of the group.

Differentiating why? This example illustrates differentiated learning and expression options within a group endeavor rather than individually. Ms. McCleary wants students with differing readiness levels, interests, and learning profiles to work together in ways that dignify each student. Thus, she has opted to use heterogeneous groups and has taken great pains to provide for individual needs and success within that context.

Figure 7.2 A Sample Complex Instruction Task Card

We have been working with how writers' lives (and ours) are often metaphors, which they (we) create through actions and deeds—including writing. We have also looked at how good authors hold up a mirror to readers, allowing readers to reflect upon their own lives and feelings. Robert Frost wrote a poem called "The Road Not Taken." Your task is to analyze the poem as a metaphor for Frost's life and as a mirror of our own. Here are the steps:

1. Find the poem, read it, interpret it, and reach consensus about what's going on in it and what it means.

2. Research Frost's life, making a "stepping stones" diagram similar to the one you created for your own life earlier this month.

3. Develop a soundscape that takes us along Frost's "journey in the woods." Use music; found sounds; sound effects; and appropriate mime, body sculpture, or narration to help your audience understand the feelings that a "journeyer in the woods" would experience as he or she came to straight places, landmarks, or decision points. Be sure you develop a script for your presentation.

4. Create an "overlay" of Frost's life and the poem, using words and images in such a way that they represent the metaphorical relationship between the two.

5. Transfer the key ideas in the poem to the life and experience of a noted person about whom we are all likely to know a little but could learn a little more. Your "transfer" must clearly draw a relationship between the person and the poem and clearly communicate to classmates how literature can help us understand ourselves.

6. Be certain that your final products demonstrate your understanding of metaphor and mirror, the relationship between varied art forms in communicating human meaning, and details of the people and poem with whom/which you are working.

As usual, you should appoint a group convener, materials monitor, recorder, and time monitor. Determine the best role for each person in your group. Remember, everyone has strengths to contribute to your group's success, and no one has all the strengths needed. Because your time is limited, you should develop a written work plan, including a time line and group conference times. Be ready to share assessment criteria for your group's work (required elements as well as your group's sense of what makes a high-quality presentation). Your group may have up to 20 minutes to make its presentation to one other group plus a 10-minute question exchange with students who serve as your audience and for whom you are an audience.

Orbital Studies

Chris Stevenson (1992, 1997) suggests orbital studies as an ideal way to address both commonalities and differences among middle-level learners. Indeed, the strategy appears easily adapted to learners at all levels. *Orbital studies* are independent investigations, generally of three to six weeks. They "orbit," or revolve, around some facet of the curriculum. Students select their own topics for orbitals, and they work with guidance and coaching from the teacher to develop more expertise both on the topic and on the process of becoming an independent investigator. Teachers can design rubrics or other criteria for success so that important knowledge, understandings, and skills from course goals are integrated into the orbital products. This allows students to pursue topics that matter to them while seeing how what they learn in class transfers to or connects with a world beyond the classroom.

Orbitals are based on the premise that all learners are dignified by developing and sharing knowledge and skills. This strategy is not unlike the merit badge system in Scouting, except that in orbital studies students develop their own topics rather than select from a prescribed list, and the topics stem from the curriculum. Stevenson (2001) suggests that initial lists of potential topics be derived from surveys of student interest and augmented by suggestions from parents and mentors (or even by perusing the Yellow Pages online or on paper).

Grade 6 (Various Subjects): Orbital Studies

Sixth graders at Hand Middle School like how orbital studies are interesting and help them be independent. Teachers also like orbitals for the way this strategy integrates the curriculum and lets them see learners at work in their areas of strength and interest.

Hand's 6th grade teachers developed a website on orbital studies, explaining to students and their families what an orbital study is, why it is important, how it works, and possible resources. Each teacher reviews the website with students in all classes in the fall, when orbitals begin, and also sends the link to students' families. The website describes general characteristics of an orbital:

• An orbital study focuses on a topic of student interest related to some facet of the curriculum.

• Important learning goals from class will be embedded in the orbital study, including key writing goals.

• A student may work on an orbital study for three to six weeks.

• Teachers help students develop a clear question for study, a plan for research, a method of presentation, and criteria for quality.

• Successfully completing an orbital includes keeping a log of time spent on the study, resources used, ideas and skills gained through the study, and how ideas and skills from class were used in the orbital. In addition, the student must make a 10- to 20-minute presentation to at least 5 peers, providing a single-page handout or visual presentation for the audience and using some sort of display or demonstration. The student also must develop and use a way to get peer feedback on the content and presentation.

Throughout the year, each teacher on the team works with individuals and small groups to help them select and focus on a topic, keep a log, find and use resource materials (including print, electronic, and human), plan and use time, measure progress against established criteria for success, make effective oral presentations, and distill key ideas for the handout or visual. This is done through mini-workshops with small groups of students who have extra time when a task is completed or via online planning sessions using apps that allow students to work with peers and check in with the teacher outside of the classroom.

All teachers assume responsibility for helping students with planning, research, time management, and presentation, but they also serve as consultants for orbitals in their own areas of interest or expertise. For example, a math teacher may be a science fiction fan, or an English teacher may know a great deal about jazz. Teachers and students alike enjoy the fact that teachers have and can share interests and skills in areas they do not teach.

A student invites a teacher to serve as consultant. Teachers generally will accept the invitation, unless they are already involved in a large number of consultations. In that case, the teacher suggests another option from the team of teachers. All teachers on the team make a special effort to help students see how orbital studies connect what is learned in class to their own talent and interest areas. They also help students see how orbitals can be used to connect various subjects. Students must complete at least one successful orbital study in a year, but may do multiple orbitals. Because the topics are personal and interesting, and because teacher support is abundant, most students keep an orbital study going much of the year.

Here is what's going on right now:

• Takisha is working on a digital "talking mural" of unsung U.S. heroes and heroines, which ties her love of art and portraiture to the study of U.S. history. She is researching little-known male and female heroes of varied races and ages who made a difference for the United States. Her mural will reflect that research. Her flair for the dramatic inspired her to write a script that she will record herself as a soundtrack for the digital mural.

• Semaj is building a rocket, which calls on him to extend his knowledge of both science and math. It also lets him use his hands in the process, an opportunity he finds too infrequently in school.

• Jake and Ellie are creating a comic book that incorporates the key elements of literature. They are developing a science fiction plot they'd like to see in literature in school.

• Lexie is working on her tennis game at a park near her house. This extension of physical education is allowing her to learn from an 8th grader who volunteered to help her improve her serve and strokes. The lessons are video recorded by a couple of her friends and her dad. Throughout the process, she compares her videos with those of professionals (provided by her physical education teacher). She ultimately will share what she has learned with peers also interested in tennis.

• David, who is passionate about soccer, is learning about countries that have been World Cup soccer champions, an extension of his studies of geography and culture.

• Louis is studying ethnic cooking, connecting studies of geography and culture. He also feels it's important to learn to cook so he can entertain friends when he gets older and has his own apartment. In the meantime, he tries out what he learns on his family and friends, and he is developing his own digital cookbook.

Much of the work on orbitals is completed at home. However, there is some time in each subject devoted to working on orbital research and related skills. Students know that when classwork is completed, they may use the extra time to work on their orbital studies. Teachers also work with the school's media specialist and art teacher to provide support and resources for students who may not find those things readily available at home. Every third Friday in one class, students present orbitals they have completed. Peers may sign up to attend a presentation in which they are interested, much like adults select sessions at a conference. All attendees provide feedback for the presenters. Students not attending a presentation may work on their own projects, catch up on missed classwork, or use the time to get peer help with some of their work.

All four of the 6th grade classrooms maintain areas designated and arranged for orbital presentations. Other areas are designated and set up for quiet work done by individuals or in pairs. If a student in the work area does not have a work plan for the class period, the teacher will provide appropriate work. When there are several orbitals ready for presentation, two classrooms are designated for presentation only, one for individual or paired work, and one for teacher assistance with work in any subject.

Following their reading and review of orbital study presentations, teachers share the summaries with other teachers on the team. The team makes a concerted effort to connect what students are learning about in their orbital studies with what they continue to learn in class. When teachers miss an opportunity—or sometimes before they seize it—students often remind them of the connections. Many of the orbital presentations are captured on video so that students in subsequent years can use them as idea generators or models of quality.

Differentiating what? Orbital studies allow differentiation of content (because students select their own topics and research materials), process (because students develop their own study plans), and product (because students can select from a wide range of options about how to express their learning). In orbital studies, content, process, and product are differentiated by student choice rather than by teacher choice. Teachers, however, play an active role in coaching students for success in understanding, preparation, and presentation and in ensuring that students apply essential content goals in their orbital work.

Differentiating how? Orbitals focus on differentiation by student interest (because of topic choice and mode of expressing learning) and learning profile (because of the opportunity to determine working conditions and/or intelligence preference). Again, the teacher assumes a key role in monitoring student choices and progress and coaching for high-quality outcomes.

Differentiating why? Students are energized by school and the learning process when it belongs to them and when they can shine in what they love to do. Orbitals allow students to exercise choice in what to study and how to share what they learn and to transfer important ideas and skills from their classes into other domains. Orbitals also provide teachers a systematic way to help young learners become more independent in their learning.

●   ●   ●

Craftsmen, whether professional or amateur, remind us that choosing the right tool for a job makes a powerful difference in the product outcome. Selecting the right instructional strategies in the classroom likewise impacts the quality of the learning experience the teacher will provide to students.

It is important to match the strategy to the requirements of the curriculum and the needs of the learner and to know whether the goal is to differentiate content, process, or product. It matters that teachers know when it makes sense to respond to learners' readiness, interest, or approach to learning and that they grasp why a particular approach will benefit the learning of particular students.

8

More Instructional Strategies to Support Differentiation

I like this class because there's something different going on all the time. My other classes, it's like peanut butter for lunch every single day. This class, it's like my teacher really knows how to cook. It's like she runs a really good restaurant with a big menu and all.

Comment from a course evaluation written by a 7th grader

There are many strategies that invite teachers to look at needs of small groups and individuals, as opposed to teaching as though all learners share the same readiness level, interests, and modes of learning. In Chapter 7, we examined stations, agendas, complex instruction, and orbital studies as tools that facilitate differentiation. In this chapter, we'll examine centers, entry points, tiered activities, learning contracts, and Tri-mind at some length. We'll also look more succinctly at small-group instruction, compacting, choice boards, and Jigsaw—all useful instructional strategies when a teacher wants to focus on individual or small-group needs within a unit or topic of study explored by all members of the class.

Centers

Teachers have used centers for many years, probably because they are flexible enough to address variable learning needs. Centers differ from stations in that they are distinct; whereas stations work in concert, centers do not. For example, a teacher may create a science center, a writing center, and an art center. But students won't need to move to all of them to achieve proficiency with a topic or set of skills. Consider the math class used to illustrate stations in Chapter 7. All students rotated among the stations to become competent with various mathematical concepts and skills. Those stations were linked in a way that centers aren't.

Different teachers use centers in different ways; thus, they define centers in different ways, too. Two kinds of centers are particularly useful for differentiated instruction: learning centers and interest centers. This section defines and offers guidance about creating these two kinds of centers, but teachers should feel free to modify the suggestions to meet their own and their students' needs.

By my definition, a *learning center* is a classroom area that contains a collection of activities or materials designed to teach, provide practice on, or extend a student's knowledge, skill, or understanding. An *interest center* is designed to motivate students' exploration of topics in which they have a particular interest. In general, centers should

- Focus on important, clearly identified learning goals;
- Contain materials that promote individual students' growth toward those goals;
- Use materials and activities addressing a wide range of reading levels, learning profiles, and student interests;
- Include activities that vary from simple to complex, concrete to abstract, and structured to open-ended;
- Provide clear directions for students;
- Offer instructions about what students should do if they need help;
- Include instructions about what students should do when they complete a center assignment;
- Use a record-keeping system to monitor what students do at the center and the quality level of their work; and

• Use formative assessment to guide development of center tasks and assignment of students to appropriate tasks.

The materials and tasks at learning centers are typically teacher-constructed, although teachers certainly can encourage students to share in designing what they will study in some centers or how students will learn at the centers. Materials and tasks can focus either on mastery or on extension of specific knowledge, understandings, or skills.

Grades 2 and 3 (Various Subjects): Dinosaur Centers

Ms. Hooper teaches in a multi-age classroom with students in Grades 2 and 3. Like most children their age, these young learners are fascinated by dinosaurs. Ms. Hooper wants to encourage their natural curiosity, but she also wants to use the study of dinosaurs to help students understand scientific concepts like patterns, classification, adaptation, and change.

Sometimes in their science study of dinosaurs, the whole class listens to a story or watches a video about dinosaurs, talks about what a dinosaur picture or skeleton can tell them if they think like scientists, or classifies a dinosaur on their classification chart. Ms. Hooper uses the science center to ensure that students get individual practice with key understandings and skills. For the next couple of weeks, all students will visit the learning center to work like paleontologists to analyze various dinosaur artifacts. As part of their center work, students will study how dinosaurs adapted to their environments. In this multi-age class, however, students vary widely in sophistication of thought and reading skill. Their previous knowledge about and interest in dinosaurs also varies.

The science learning center contains plastic figures of dinosaurs; pictures of dinosaurs; fossils of bones, teeth, skin, and footprints; replicas of dinosaur skeletons; several books; and some coloring book outlines of dinosaurs. It also includes a variety of art materials and writing tools. Directions are written on cards and recorded on a small digital recorder. Students know they are assigned to the center when they see their name on a chart titled "Paleontologists of the Day."

Ms. Hooper provides written and digitally recorded directions in the center to guide student work. The work generally entails examining and making observations about artifacts. At the science learning center, all students will be working with the concept of patterns, the skills of classifying and predicting, and the understanding that examining patterns in nature helps us make good predictions. Students will be assigned to this center on several occasions over two weeks. They also may elect to visit the center when it is not in use and when they have student choice time. Students who work with basic tasks at the beginning of the two weeks may later work with tasks that more advanced students completed earlier in the study.

Among today's visiting paleontologists are Gina, almost 9, and Jordan, who is a young 7. Both find reading difficult, and, at this point, they need highly structured learning tasks. Their artifact box contains two models of dinosaur teeth and three plastic models of dinosaurs. They are asked to examine the teeth to predict what the animal eats, then look at the legs, necks, and hands of the three models and predict what these features suggest (see Figure 8.1). Finally, they are to select another dinosaur model from the center and make predictions by examining its features. The digital recorder can help guide their reading if they choose to use it. Also, to provide more support for their work at the center, Ms. Hooper has assigned Gina and Jordan to work together.

On another day, Mishea, an 8-year-old, and Carla, who is still 6, are working on a similar task, one that Ms. Hooper has designed to respond to their advanced reading and classification skills and their large store of knowledge about dinosaurs. Directions are, again, available on the digital recorder. Their artifact box contains fossils of skeletons, bones, and teeth, as well as a number of pictures of dinosaurs labeled with their names. These students, like Gina and Jordan, must use the artifacts to make predictions about dinosaur adaptation. Their task sheet (see Figure 8.2), which asks them to "think like a paleontologist," reflects the greater complexity and less-structured nature of their assignment.

In addition to the science learning center, there are two skills-based learning centers and one interest center in Ms. Hooper's classroom. In one learning center, students work on math skills via a computer-based program that monitors their progress, provides assistance as needed, and escalates task difficulty as students are ready to move ahead. This program is particularly useful for students who need to "work backwards" to master math skills and thinking from previous units or years in school, and it also provides practice with current math skills. As students demonstrate mastery of current skills, they work with a program that uses increasingly complex problems to challenge students in applying and extending what they have learned in multiple areas of math.

Figure 8.1 A More Structured Science Center Task: Dinosaur Worksheets

1. The green dinosaur is a Hypsilaphodon.

It has a _____ neck.
         long/short

It is good for _____ .
  eating leaves from tall trees/eating short bushes

It has _____ legs.
  long and thin/short and chunky

They are for _____ .
      walking slowly/running fast

To protect itself this dinosaur uses _____ .
     claws/spikes/running/club tail

It uses its long tail _____ .
        to swim/for balance

2. The gray dinosaur is Triceratops.

It has a _____ neck, pointy teeth, and a beak.
     long/short

They are good for _____ .
     eating soft leaves from tall trees/
        eating tough low plants

It has _____ legs.
    short and chunky/
    long and thin

They are good for _____ .
    walking slowly/running

To protect itself, this dinosaur uses _____ .
        running/claws/
        horn/a club tail

3. The brown dinosaur is Euoplocephalus.

It has good legs for _____ .
     running fast/walking

It has a beak, which means it probably
eats _____ .
    plants/animals

To protect itself it uses _____ .
     running/club tail/
     armor/bony spikes

4. Pick another dinosaur and tell about it. Draw it if you'd like to.

Figure 8.2 A Less Structured Science Center Task: I Can Think Like a Paleontologist

Dinosaur	Legs	Tail	Teeth	Other Trait
Hypsilophodon	Kind For	Kind For	Kind For	Kind For
Triceratops	Kind For	Kind For	Kind For	Kind For
Euoplocephalus	Kind For	Kind For	Kind For	Kind For
Tyrannosaurus	Kind For	Kind For	Kind For	Kind For
Stegosaurus	Kind For	Kind For	Kind For	Kind For
Your Choice (Give Name)	Kind For	Kind For	Kind For	Kind For

In the language arts center, students use graphic organizers and informational texts to find main ideas and supporting details. Right now, the class's readings focus on dinosaurs so that students are using text structure to extend their knowledge about a topic they are excited to learn about together. Ms. Hooper matches both print and Internet sources at different levels of text complexity to address students' varied reading levels. She also includes sources in other languages to support students whose first language is not English.

The interest center on dinosaurs encourages students to enrich and expand their understanding of topics related to their formal study. Students may sign up to go to the center during student choice time, but they are not required to do so. They also may elect to work alone or with a partner. This center has several tasks proposed by Ms. Hooper and a wide range of art, print, and video materials useful for completing the tasks. The tasks posted at the interest center this week include the following:

• Find out how iguanas are like dinosaurs and draw a comparison picture with labels.

• Read about Chinese dragons and other mythological creatures that may have been inspired by dinosaurs. Share what you learn with the class on our science blog.

• Make a dinosaur skeleton from clay and plastic bones to show how the dinosaur is adapted to its environment.

• Find out three things scientists think might have caused the extinction of dinosaurs. Make posters to tell the class about the three ideas.

• Find out about today's reptiles that are relatives of dinosaurs. Make drawings or models that compare them to dinosaurs. Use labels to show what is alike.

• Write a job description for a paleontologist that explains what the person does and what kind of training is needed.

Students also can design their own task by completing an "I Want to Know" planning form and presenting it to the teacher (see Figure 8.3).

Differentiating what? In the learning centers, Ms. Hooper differentiates materials (a part of content) while ensuring that all students practice essential concepts and skills. She also differentiates process as she provides activities at varied levels of complexity. At the interest center, Ms. Hooper differentiates content by giving students choices about what to study. She differentiates

Figure 8.3 A Student-Designed Interest Center Task Template: I Want to Know

My question or topic is _____

_____

_____

_____

To find out about it, I will _____

I will look at and listen to:

I will read:

I will draw:

I will write:

I will need:

I will finish by_____

I will share what I learned by

_____

_____

_____

process by varying the ways students learn. She differentiates product by offering varied options for students to demonstrate their learning.

Differentiating how? Using the learning centers allows Ms. Hooper to differentiate instruction by student readiness level; she varies the complexity of resources and tasks to match students' starting points. Interest centers focus on a variety of student interests, and they include the option for students to propose their own studies. In both learning centers and interest centers, the teacher can attend to learning profile differences by having students work alone or with peers; presenting visual and auditory directions; and providing resources that contribute to kinesthetic, visual, spatial, and linguistic strengths.

Differentiating why? In a multi-age primary classroom, differences in readiness, background knowledge, interest, and learning profile are evident, although not necessarily by age or grade. By having students work together, individually, and in small groups, the teacher creates community learning experiences while also attending to individual needs. By sometimes having students work on the same learning center tasks at different points in time, Ms. Hooper's planning is made easier. She also effectively escalates student growth. Further, there is a balance between student choice and teacher choice in use of centers. The teacher makes key assignments to the learning centers, but students may elect to return to a learning center. They initiate their own involvement with the interest center.

Entry Points

Howard Gardner (1993) has contributed greatly to the awareness that students vary in intelligence preferences or strengths. Through his continuing investigation of different approaches to learning, he has helped educators understand that a child who is quite strong spatially may prefer to take in information, solve problems, and express learning differently than a child whose strength is more oriented to language, for example. Although Gardner is clear that intelligences are interrelated, and that all of us use a variety of intelligences in our everyday lives, he also is convinced that there are important differences among the intelligences and that attending to students' differences as learners can facilitate learning. Teachers can support learning by making room or allowing for these differences when planning and carrying out instruction.

Gardner (1991, 1993) describes "entry points," or avenues of learning, as a strategy for addressing varied intelligence preferences. He proposes student exploration of a given topic thorough varied entry points:

• *Narrational entry point:* Presenting a story or narrative about the topic or concept in question.

• *Logical-quantitative entry point:* Using numbers or deductive/scientific approaches to the topic or question.

• *Foundational entry point:* Examining the philosophy and vocabulary that undergird the topic or concept.

• *Aesthetic entry point:* Focusing on the sensory features of the topic or concept.

• *Experiential entry point:* Using a hands-on approach where the student deals directly with materials that represent the topic or concept. These materials also make links to the student's personal experience.

Grade 7 History: Entry Points to the Middle Ages

Ms. Boutchard and her 7th grade students are about to begin an exploration of the Middle Ages in Europe. She has decided to introduce the culture and thought of the time by having students investigate cathedrals. A medieval cathedral is an exemplar—almost a metaphor—for much of the time period. She believes students will have a far richer platform for understanding the period and its people if they understand the technology used in building cathedrals, what it meant to be an architect during that time, the raw materials that were available, the occupational system that supported the crafting and construction of these amazing structures, and the belief system that made them so important.

Students in Ms. Boutchard's class begin their focus on the Middle Ages with a whole-class discussion of what they think of when they hear that term. This gives students a chance to link previous understandings with the learning to come. It gives their teacher a chance to informally get a sense of students' level and depth of knowledge about the time period.

She then gives each student a choice of "signing on" to any one of the five entry point investigations (see the overviews in Figure 8.4). Students may elect to work alone or in a group of up to four. The teacher also has developed an assignment sheet for each investigation, including specific criteria for success.

Figure 8.4 A Capsule Overview of Entry Point Investigation Options

Entry Point	Project Title	Assignment
Narrational	Cathedrals Tell Stories	Use stories provided by the teacher or find others in which a cathedral is an important feature (almost a character) in the plot. Develop a glossary of terms about a cathedral from information in the story (not from a dictionary or encyclopedia). Show through drawings and supporting written explanations how the author(s) used the cathedral to help shape the story. Write or orally tell a tale or adventure of your own in which you use the cathedral as a "central figure" in the story.
Logical-quantitative	Builders of a Legacy	Using resources suggested by the teacher and other materials you may find, develop a model that shows the key features of a cathedral and the kind of engineering knowledge and skills the builders used to construct them. It's important to think about knowledge and skill available to engineers now in comparison to those of the Middle Ages.
Foundational	It All Means Something	Cathedrals are full of symbols. Find a way to show and explain how the floor plan, art, decorations, and other elements help us understand the beliefs of the people who built and worshiped in cathedrals in the Middle Ages. The teacher has provided resource materials for a starting point. You'll probably want to find others as well.
Aesthetic	Beauty in the Eye of the Beholder	Using resource materials provided by the teacher and others you may find, develop a way to show how the architecture, art, and music of the cathedral tell us what people of the Middle Ages thought was beautiful and why. You may find it useful to compare their beliefs about beauty with some of our own time period.
Experiential	Your "Cathedral"	Most of us have "places" that make us pause, think, wonder, or feel at peace. Some of these are places of worship built by architects and engineers. Others are simple places that take on special meaning to our lives. Using the list of elements of a cathedral and resources on cathedrals provided by the teacher, find a way to show either one or more of your "cathedrals" or someone else's that you know about. Help the class see how the "cathedrals" you select are like cathedrals in the Middle Ages in important ways.

Once the entry points investigations are complete, Ms. Boutchard will build on the students' work throughout the unit that follows.

Differentiating what? Ms. Boutchard differentiates content by providing a range of research resources for each group to support varied reading proficiencies. She differentiates process by providing varied ways to think about cathedrals. The products students create will show what they have learned in varied forms. What stays the same for all students is the need to think about what a cathedral is and what it reveals about the people and the time it represents.

Differentiating how? Interest and learning profile are the predominant emphases of differentiation. Students can select the investigation that seems most intriguing to them, specialize in an area of intelligence preference, select working conditions, and make many choices about how to express what they learn. The teacher supports some readiness differentiation by initially providing resource materials at a range of reading levels.

Differentiating why? By introducing a topic of study through various intelligence- and interest-based lenses, Ms. Boutchard taps into student strengths and prior experiences. Thus, she enhances motivation, success, and understanding of the same subject among students whose learning profiles and interests differ in important ways. Despite the different modes of learning, however, each student comes away from the entry point investigations with some common understandings of the time period and people of the Middle Ages. This will help them connect and make sense of facts, concepts, and principles in the rest of the unit.

Tiered Activities

Tiered activities are useful when a teacher wants to ensure that students with different degrees of learning proficiency work with the same essential ideas and use the same key knowledge and skills. In other words, tiering is a readiness-based strategy. For example, a student who struggles with reading or has a difficult time with abstract thinking nonetheless needs to make sense of the pivotal concepts and principles in a given article or story. A student who is advanced well beyond grade expectations in that same subject needs to find genuine challenge in working with the same key content. A one-size-fits-all activity is unlikely to help either struggling or grade-level learners come to own important ideas, nor will it extend the understanding of students with great knowledge and skill in the area.

Using tiered activities allows all students to focus on essential knowledge, understandings, and skills, but at different levels of complexity, abstractness, open-endedness, and independence. By keeping the focus of the activity the same but providing routes of access at varying degrees of difficulty, the teacher maximizes the likelihood that each student comes away with pivotal skills and understandings and all students are appropriately challenged.

Here are the steps for developing a tiered activity (see also Figure 8.5).

1. Select the knowledge, understandings (concepts, generalizations), and skills that will be the focus of the activity for all learners. These are the elements the teacher knows are essential to helping students build a framework of meaning.

2. Think about the students for whom you are planning the activity. Use formative assessment (e.g., exit cards, journal entries, homework, class activities) related to the upcoming lesson to help you understand students' range of readiness for the topic. Add to that your awareness of students' particular strengths, approaches to learning, and interests. This need not be an involved process. Think of it as an outgrowth of persistent formative assessment and informal study of students.

3. Create an activity, or draw on one you've successfully used in the past. It should be interesting, require high-level thought, and clearly focus on elements that will cause students to use key skills to understand a key idea. Although you may begin planning at any number of starting points, it's wise to begin by creating an advanced task. "Teaching up" is far more likely to benefit a very broad range of students than is beginning with a more basic-level task and making adjustments from that point. When you design an assignment for advanced students first and then create versions of the task with varied degrees of scaffolding to support other students, you're more likely to provide all students with a rich, complex learning experience that's focused on meaning-making and understanding.

4. Chart the complexity of the activity. Think about, or actually draw, a ladder. The top rung represents students with very high skill and high complexity of understanding of the topic. The bottom rung represents students with low skill and low complexity of understanding of the topic. Where would your lesson be on the ladder? In other words, will it really stretch your most advanced students? Is it likely to challenge grade-level students or only those whose skills and understanding are currently at a more fundamental level? Once you visualize this kind of ladder, you can see who needs another version of the lesson. Again, "teaching up" is the most promising approach to tiering.

5. "Clone" the activity along the ladder to provide different versions at different degrees of difficulty. There is no magic number of versions.

Figure 8.5 Developing a Tiered Activity

1 Select the activity organizer
- concept
- skill
- generalization/understanding

Essential to building a framework for meaning

2 Think about your students or use assessments
- readiness range
- interests
- learning profile
- talents

- skills
- reading
- thinking
- information
- language

3 Create an activity that
- is interesting
- is high level
- causes students to use key skill(s) to understand a key idea
- allows you to "teach up"

4 Chart the complexity of the activity

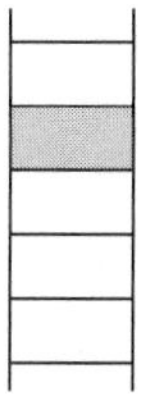

High skill or complexity

Low skill or complexity

5 Clone the activity along the ladder, as needed, to ensure challenge and success for students, assessing it in terms of
- materials—basic to advanced
- form of expression—from familiar to unfamiliar
- form of experience—from personal to removed from personal
- the Equalizer*

6 Match a version of the task to a student, based on student profile and task requirements

* See the Appendix, p. 185

Sometimes two will do. Sometimes three, four, or even five may work better to reach a wide range of learners. Formative assessment should reveal patterns of student need that guide your decision about the number of tiers appropriate for a particular task on a particular day. Cloning occurs when you vary materials students will use, from very basic to challenging for even the most advanced students, and when you allow students to express their learning in ways that range from very familiar to unfamiliar. It occurs when you develop a range of applications, from those that closely relate to students' experiences to those that are far removed. (See the Appendix for a discussion of "the Equalizer," which can be very helpful in thinking about the cloning process.)

6. Match a version of the task to each student based on his or her needs and the task requirements. The goal is to match the task's degree of difficulty and pacing to student readiness. The goal should be to stretch all students slightly beyond their comfort zone and to provide the support necessary for students to succeed at the new level of challenge.

Grade 8 Science: Tiered Activities on Ozone

Mrs. Lightner's 8th grade students are studying the atmosphere. They have had class discussions, read text materials, viewed videos, and completed a whole-class activity. It is essential that all students understand what ozone is and why it is important in the atmosphere. Mrs. Lightner wants each student to create a foundation for constructing additional knowledge and understanding of the topic.

To develop a challenging tiered activity, Mrs. Lightner consulted her most recent assessment of student understanding and considered what she knows about her students' reading levels and thinking profiles. Based on her sense of student needs, she "cloned" an activity on ozone that she had used previously and matched the various versions to individual students. The four versions of the new tiered activity all contain the same core elements:

• All students will have some individual and some group tasks to complete.

• All students will receive a packet of printed material on what ozone is, how it works, and why it is important. The reading level of the various packets varies, however, from below grade level to college-level readability.

• All students will be required to take notes on essential information in the packets. Mrs. Lightner gives some students a note-taking matrix to guide their work; others, she simply asks to take careful notes on a list of key ideas. She monitors all student notes for clarity and thoroughness.

• All students will use the Internet to expand their understanding of the importance of ozone. Mrs. Lightner directs students to a variety of websites that vary in complexity: some providing basic information; some used by practicing professionals; some in between; some with more diagrams or photographs or spoken narration; and some in Spanish, the first language of a number of students in her classes. In addition, she encourages the class to find other useful Internet sites and to share them with classmates through a designated "bulletin board" on the class website. All students are expected to appropriately cite their sources and to add to their notes what they learn from the Internet resources.

• To demonstrate understanding of what ozone is and why it is important, each student will work with one or two others to complete the same version of an activity. They will draw upon the Internet resources and their notes to apply what they have learned.

• All students have a meaningful audience for their work.

For example, Mrs. Lightner asks the group having the most difficulty with the concept to write a public service announcement about the health hazards of ozone depletion. The students use jingles, slogans, and art to convey their ideas about why ozone matters, how its depletion puts them at risk, and what they should do to take precautions. Their public service announcements are designed for the school's video newscast and its audience of elementary students.

A group with a bit more skill in reading and comprehending this type of scientific material independently conducts a survey of peer awareness and understanding about ozone. They use a professionally constructed survey to serve as a model for designing, conducting, analyzing, and reporting their own survey. Mrs. Lightner indicates the number of questions they can ask and the number of students they can poll, to make the task manageable and focus it on essential issues. Like the first group, their findings will be used for the school's newscast; they have a choice whether to present their results as graphics, storyboards, or a series of charts. Whatever format they select has to convey both findings and implications.

Students in a third group, who are generally at or slightly above grade level in this area, will write a position paper, also for the school's newscast, on the degree to which human activity may or may not negatively impact the ozone cycle. All viewpoints have to be supported with credible evidence.

A fourth group of students will debate the issue of whether there is an ozone problem to which humans contribute. Each debater represents a specific environmental or political organization, with a particular set of beliefs. All debaters have to reflect the viewpoint of their organization and simultaneously refute or respond to opposing perspectives in a point/counterpoint presentation format in which students both propose important understandings about ozone and respond to opposing points made by other students. They will practice their debates before appearing on the school's newscast.

Differentiating what? Mrs. Lightner differentiates content by presenting students with reference materials at differing readability levels and suggesting varying Internet sites. What she does not differentiate is the essential understanding of what ozone is and why it is important to living things. She differentiates process by varying the amount of support she provides for note taking and the level of complexity, abstractness, and multifaceted nature of student demonstrations of understanding. What she does not differentiate in process is the need for all students to use print and Internet resources, distill information, develop and apply understandings, and share with peers what they have learned.

Differentiating how? A tiered lesson focuses primarily on readiness differentiation. However, the teacher also can address interest or learning profile differentiation by encouraging students to propose alternate forms of expressing what they learn, varying group size, allowing students to work alone, providing recordings of resource materials, or varying time allowed for the tasks.

Differentiating why? Mrs. Lightner has two key goals in developing this tiered activity. First, she wants all students to have a real understanding of what ozone is and how its presence or absence affects their world. Second, she wants them all to work hard in order to succeed with achieving and demonstrating those understandings. The carefully focused tiered activity maximizes the chance the two goals will be realized for each student in the class. A side benefit to the tiered activity is that while students are busy with their research and application, she is free to work with small groups on reading, comprehension, scientific writing, use of the Internet, or note taking.

Learning Contracts and Contract-Like Strategies

There are many approaches to using learning contracts and contract-like strategies, but each approach includes an opportunity for students to work somewhat independently on material that is largely, but not necessarily solely, teacher-assigned based on formative assessment information related to content included on the contract. In essence, a learning contract is a negotiated agreement between teacher and student that gives students some freedom in acquiring designated knowledge, skills, and understandings that a teacher deems important at a given time. Many learning contracts and other contract-like strategies also provide opportunities for student choice regarding some of what is to be learned, working conditions, and/or how essential content will be applied or expressed. Contracts may take the form of learning contracts, Think-Tac-Toe, learning tickets, Bingos (in which students must complete a horizontal, vertical, or diagonal set of tasks from a grid), learning menus, learning agendas, or other formats.

Regardless of format, a contract or contract-like strategy generally

• Assumes it is the teacher's responsibility to specify important content goals and make sure students work with them in a way that moves the student forward;

• Assumes students can take on some of the responsibility for guiding their own learning;

• Delineates knowledge or skills that need to be practiced and mastered;

• Ensures students will apply or use those skills in context (in other words, use the knowledge and skill to explore or extend an important understanding);

• Specifies the working conditions students must adhere to during the contract time (e.g., student responsibilities, time constraints, and homework and classwork involvement);

• Sets positive consequences (continued opportunity to work independently) when students adhere to working conditions and establishes negative consequences (teacher makes work assignments and sets working parameters) if students do not adhere to working conditions;

• Establishes criteria for the completion and quality of work; and

• Includes both teacher and student signatures of agreement to the contract's terms.

Grade 4 Language Arts: Learning Contracts for Poetry Study

Ms. Howe and her 4th graders are studying poetry. During the course of the three-week language arts unit, students will work with concepts such as rhyme, imagery, word choice, and sensory description. They will work with the following key principles:

- Poetry helps readers understand and appreciate their world.
- Poetry uses precise, powerful language.
- Poetry helps readers see and think about the world around them.

Students will practice skills such as use of rhyming words, elaboration of images and ideas, making metaphors, and punctuation.

Sometimes, Ms. Howe uses whole-class instruction to introduce terms (e.g., *metaphor, simile, rhyme*) and to acquaint students with poetic forms (e.g., clerihews, cinquains, haiku, acrostics). The class as a whole also works together to explore poets' works and to "test" the unit's principles. Sometimes all students work with the same activity, such as an exercise on creating similes that describe people and things in the classroom. At other times, they work on a similar activity, such as a paired practice in which students add punctuation to poems; in this case, Ms. Howe varies the poems she assigns based on complexity of the poem, the punctuation task, and student skill with interpreting poetry and with punctuation.

A major part of the poetry unit is completed through a learning contract. Ms. Howe's students use two different learning contracts (see Figures 8.6 and 8.7). Both have similar but not always identical headings in the cells on the grid. Both include an abbreviated explanation of a task that must be completed during the course of the poetry unit. Both also invite student ownership and feedback by encouraging students to develop their own tasks or repeat those they especially like. The learning contract categories match a filing system in the classroom for students' completed work.

Three times a week during the unit, students have a contract period when they work with their contract grid. Students check off the circles and squares as they complete their work, but those icons have an additional use. Students for whom writing and interpreting poetry is new or more difficult use the contract with the circles (Figure 8.6). Students who are ready for advanced work with poetry use the contract with the squares (Figure 8.7).

Figure 8.6 A Poetry Contract

Create a Rhyming Wheel ◯ Use your spelling lists as a way to get started.	**Use Your Rhyming Wheel** ◯ Write a poem that sounds like Shel Silverstein might have written it.	**Write an Acrostic Poem** ◯ Be sure it includes alliteration.
Write ◯ A cinquain (check with another cinquain writer to make sure you got the pattern).	**Computer Art** ◯ Use clip art to illustrate a simile, a metaphor, or an analogy on our class list or one that you come up with yourself.	**Write About You** ◯ Use good descriptive words in a poem to help us know and understand something important about you.
Interpret ◯ "How to Eat a Poem."	**Research a Famous Person** ◯ Take notes, using the biography graphic organizer.	**Illustrate a Poem** ◯ Find a poem you like that we've read or that you have read on your own. Illustrate it. Write about why you illustrated it as you did.
Student Choice #1 ◯ _____ _____ _____	**Student Choice #2** ◯ _____ _____ _____	**Student Choice #3** ◯ _____ _____ _____

Figure 8.7 A Second Poetry Contract

Create a Rhyming Wheel ☐ Use your spelling lists and a dictionary as a way to get started.	**Use Your Rhyming Wheel** ☐ Write a poem about something that makes you laugh or smile.	**Write an Acrostic Poem** ☐ Be sure it includes alliteration and onomatopoeia.
Write ☐ A diamante (check with another diamante writer to make sure you got the pattern).	**Computer Art** ☐ Use clip art to illustrate a simile, a metaphor, or an analogy you come up with.	**Write About You** ☐ Use good description, figurative language, and images to write a poem that helps us understand something important about you.
Interpret ☐ "Unfolding Bud."	**Research a Famous Person** ☐ Take notes in an organized way. Write a bio-poem that uses what you learned.	**Illustrate a Poem** ☐ Find a poem you like that we have not read in class. Illustrate the poem in a way that helps the reader understand its meaning. Write about why you illustrated it as you did.
Student Choice #1 ☐ _____ _____ _____	**Student Choice #2** ☐ _____ _____ _____	**Student Choice #3** ☐ _____ _____ _____

The use of different symbols makes it easier for the teacher to see at a glance which contract is which. Students seem unconcerned about or unaware of the use of different symbols.

Ms. Howe grades students on the contract portion of the unit in three ways. First, students get a grade based on how well they worked (i.e., had a goal, worked steadily toward it, adhered to working conditions). Second, the teacher spot-checks one or two assignments from each student's grid for completion, accuracy, and quality. Third, each student selects two pieces to become part of the class electronic portfolio on poetry, which are assessed by the student, a peer, and the teacher according to a quality checklist posted in the class for each type of poem. Students may revise their work based on peer and teacher feedback before submitting it for inclusion in the portfolio. Portfolio pieces also include a student reflection on the work and may include drawings or photographs that relate to the work.

Both versions of the contract give students experience practicing discrete skills such as working with figures of speech and interpreting a poem. They also offer students the chance to incorporate those skills in creating poetry. Variations in the cells address readiness differences. For example, writing a cinquain is more straightforward than writing a diamante; Eve Merriam's "How to Eat a Poem" is more concrete than Naoshi Koriyama's "Unfolding Bud," even though, in both cases, students are interpreting poems about poetry.

Another way the teacher addresses readiness differences is through directions. For example, directions that accompany the contract with the circles ask students to read "How to Eat a Poem," illustrate it, summarize what it says, and write about what it means or what others can learn from it. Directions accompanying the contract with the squares ask students to read "Unfolding Bud," paraphrase it, and explain what it helps the reader understand about a poet and his or her poetry. Students also are asked to write a similar poem about poetry, or some other subject, that uses metaphor as poets do.

Ms. Howe's students are enthusiastic about the freedom and responsibility they have in planning a time line to complete their work, making choices about what to do on which day, and deciding what goes in the empty grid cells. Ms. Howe enjoys the freedom the contract period gives her to have individual conferences with students on poetry or on other facets of their work that need her attention.

Differentiating what? Contracts allow the teacher to differentiate content (kinds of poems to be written and interpreted, resource materials) and process (varying directions). Still, all students work with the same essential concepts and skills.

Differentiating how? As used by Ms. Howe, contracts allow differentiation by readiness (different poems, directions, materials), interest (student choice cells), and learning profile (students making decisions about when and how to work on tasks).

Differentiating why? Contracts allow students to engage with poetry at a level of sophistication that enhances the likelihood that each student will feel challenged and successful. Further, the balance of whole-class instruction and contract work offers a good mix of teacher direction and student-centeredness.

Tri-mind

Tri-mind is based on the work of Robert Sternberg (1985, 1988, 1997), who proposes three "intelligences," or modes of processing, that all functional human beings possess and use in daily life, while also suggesting that many people will have preferences for or strengths in one or two of the intelligences rather than in all three. The three intelligences are *analytical intelligence* ("schoolhouse" intelligence, characterized by part-to-whole, linear, and sequential ways of learning), *practical intelligence* (real-world-application learning, characterized by use of knowledge in authentic contexts), and *creative intelligence* (characterized by imaginative problem solving, innovation, and thinking outside the box in useful ways). Allowing students to learn and express learning in preferred areas increases achievement (Grigorenko & Sternberg, 1997; Sternberg, Torff, & Grigorenko, 1998).

Using Tri-mind in the classroom typically begins with delineating which learning goals the activity should help students master. The teacher then develops an analytical task, a practical task, and a creative task (or options for each category) that will result in students achieving the goals regardless of task choice. As with all significant work, students should understand the task, working conditions for the task, targeted learning goals, and criteria for success. Tri-mind is especially well suited for differentiation in response to students' learning profiles, but Tri-mind activities also can be adjusted to address students' readiness- and interest-based needs.

Grade 10 Biology: Tri-mind Tasks for Studying the Human Cell

Mr. Alvero and his biology students have been working for about a week on the structure and function of a human cell. Now that they have some background on the topic, he has developed a Tri-mind task to help his students reflect on the interdependent nature of a cell. As a result of the task, he wants his students to know the names and functions of cell parts; understand that a cell is a system with interrelated parts; and be able to analyze the interrelationships of cell parts and functions and present their understanding in a clear, useful, interesting, and fresh way.

He introduces the tasks by noting that sometimes people learn best in ways that seem most natural or useful to them. He explains that because the students are likely to be the best judge of which approach to learning will be most effective for them, they will be able to choose from among several options as the class explores an important idea. He points out that the learning goals are identical for each task.

Mr. Alvero's list of tasks (see Figure 8.8) includes one analytical task, one practical task, and two creative tasks (one that emphasizes visual or tactile creativity and another option that emphasizes verbal creativity). He feels there are students in his classes who would gravitate to one of the creative options but not the other.

Mr. Alvero is amazed as he watches the students work. They are fully engaged, and their ideas capture the key understandings for the task clearly and in a broad variety of ways. He is particularly interested in some of the work done by students who selected the more tactile creative task. Whereas some students use small items to depict the cell, others use large objects such as furniture. Still others who chose that task use their peers to create a model of the cell and explain its function, making analogies between the cell parts and the roles their classmates tend to play in the class or school.

When students have completed their work, he has them share in two small-group contexts—first with two other students who did the same task they did and then with two other students who did other tasks. He finds that students seem to gain a deeper sense of understanding when sharing in the first group and a broader sense of understanding as a result of sharing in the second group. Later in the year, Mr. Alvero notes that he has never had a year in which his students understood the structure and function of the cell so well, retained it so long, or were able to transfer insights about it to other systems they studied later in the course.

Figure 8.8 A Biology Tri-mind Assignment

Name _____

We have been studying the structure and function of a human cell. To explore the interdependent nature of the parts of a cell, select from one of the options listed below.

Option 1 (Analytical)	Use a cause/effect chain or some other format you develop to show how each part of a cell affects other parts as well as the whole. Use labels, directional markers, and other symbols as appropriate to ensure that someone who is pretty clueless about how a cell works will be enlightened after studying your work.
Option 2 (Practical)	Look around you in your world or the broader world for systems that could serve as analogies for the cell. Select your best analogy ("best" meaning most clearly matched, most explanatory or enlightening). Devise a way to make the analogy clear and visible to an audience of your peers, ensuring that they will develop clearer and richer insights about how a cell works by sharing in your work. Be sure to emphasize both the individual functions of cell parts and the interrelationships among the parts.
Option 3 (Creative—Spatial, Tactile)	Use unlikely "stuff" in our classroom to depict the structure and function of the cell, with emphasis on interrelationships among each of the parts. You should select your materials carefully to reveal something important about the cell, its parts, and their interrelationships. Your "aha!"s should trigger ours.
Option 4 (Creative—Verbal)	Tell a story that helps us understand a cell as a system with interdependent actors or characters, a plot to carry out, a setting, and even a potential conflict. Use your own imagination and narrative preferences to help us gain insights into the interdependence of the parts in this remarkable system.

Differentiating what? In this lesson, Mr. Alvero differentiated process —an opportunity for his students to make sense of the parts of a cell and their interrelationship in the system of a cell.

Differentiating how? The Tri-mind strategy allows students to approach learning in varied ways. Therefore, it's a strategy designed to address students' learning profile preferences.

Differentiating why? Mr. Alvero wanted to offer his students a choice about how they made sense of and shared ideas about the cell as a system. Because all three approaches led to the same learning outcomes, rather than assigning one of the three approaches to students, he asked them to select the approach they found most interesting. Students felt free to work in a way that seemed fun or intriguing, and they benefited from sharing their experiences both with peers who selected the same approach and with peers who elected to work in the other two ways.

Other Strategies That Invite Differentiation

A myriad of instructional and management strategies invite teachers to break classes into smaller learning units. Although all units call for whole-class learning, at times subdividing the class based on students' readiness, interests, and approaches to learning enables the teacher to think about variation in student needs. These groupings should ensure that all students work with engaging, high-level tasks focused squarely on essential content and that they work regularly with a wide variety of peers.

The following are just a few of the many strategies that invite differentiation. Add your own favorite strategies to the list. This list should be endless; it should grow as we become more expert at creating academically responsive classrooms. In fact, it's often the case that the strategies teachers invent are better suited to their students and content areas than the strategies they borrow from other sources.

Small-Group Instruction

A powerful strategy for addressing students' varied learning needs is the use of small groups for teaching, practice, or discussion. When a teacher's classroom observations and formative assessment indicate that some students are lagging behind in key content proficiency, lack prerequisite content, have misunderstandings about how the content works, or are advanced with essential content, small-group instruction provides a simple and direct way to reteach, review, provide focused and supervised practice, clarify misunderstandings, or extend student proficiency. Small groups are also useful in making interest-based connections with essential knowledge, understanding, and skill.

Some students simply learn better and participate more actively in small, teacher-led groups than in the class as a whole. Use of small groups can also be a helpful source of formative assessment for the teacher. Small-group sessions don't need to be long, but they need to be focused on the next steps in learning for particular students so that students are able to move ahead in their knowledge, understanding, and skill more effectively and efficiently as a result of their participation in the small-group setting. It's also important for students who are not in the small-group setting at a given time to know how to work productively on meaningful work while the teacher is occupied with others, including how to get help when the teacher is not available and what to do if they complete their work before the class reconvenes.

Compacting

Compacting, or *curriculum compacting* (Reis, Burns, & Renzulli, 1992), encourages teachers to assess students before beginning a unit of study or development of a skill. Students who do well on the pre-assessment (getting as much as three-quarters correct) should not have to continue to work on what they already know. With three-stage compacting, teachers document (1) what students already know (and evidence for that conclusion), (2) what the pre-assessment indicates students do not know about the topic or skill (and plans for how they will learn those things), and (3) a plan for meaningful and challenging use of the time students will "buy" because they already know much of the topic or skill. Compacting begins with a focus on student readiness and ends with an emphasis on student interest.

Choice Boards

Choice boards are well suited to dealing with readiness and interest differences among students. Teachers place changing assignments in permanent pockets on choice boards; by asking a student to make a work selection from a particular row, the teacher targets work toward student need and at the same time allows student choice. For young nonreaders, cards can be coded with icons or colors. For older students, the cards may use words to designate a task or area of the room. In either case, full instructions for the task are given at the place the student works, not on the choice board itself. Put another way, the choice board simply allows the teacher to "direct traffic."

Literature and Discussion Circles

Literature circles (Daniels, 2002) are a student-centered approach to discussing fiction in which students meet in small groups to talk about what they are reading. This strategy is designed to enhance student understanding of the piece of literature; to develop skills in the areas of comprehension, text analysis, and oral expression; and to shift leadership of meaningful discussions from teacher to students. Typically, students select the books they will read and discuss, so books and discussions will vary across groups. Each student plays a key role (e.g., discussion facilitator, summarizer, connector, vocabulary builder, text finder) in the literature circle, and roles rotate within a circle over a period of time. Students receive descriptions of role expectations and parameters for the discussions. The idea of literature circles is easily adaptable to any subject area or kind of text. It is flexible; teachers can assign texts or allow student choice of texts (although choice is an important aspect of the original conception), rotate roles or assign roles based on student interests and strengths, and so on.

Jigsaw

Jigsaw (www.jigsaw.org) is a three-stage collaborative strategy:

1. The teacher introduces students to a topic or idea the Jigsaw groups will explore and establishes the working directions and conditions for the groups, so that students will know what they will need to do for the Jigsaw to succeed.

2. Students meet in "home base" groups where they examine directions and materials for the upcoming task; groups will work together as a team to learn about the aspects of the topic assigned to them. Each group should have roughly the same number of students, and the overall task needs to have as many parts as there are students in the group. (If some groups have an additional member, then two members of that group work with the same topic.) Once students in the home base groups are clear on their goals and work, they divide into "expert groups" (or "study groups"). In the expert groups, students use print, video, or electronic resources to find out about their topic or question. Members of an expert group ultimately discuss what they have learned, sharing information and insights so that each member benefits from the work of other members as well as from his or her own work.

3. Students in the expert groups return to their home base groups and share what they have learned with peers who have learned about other aspects of the topic. It's often helpful for students to have mechanisms for recording, organizing, and reflecting on what they learn from their own work as well as that of their peers and for the teacher to follow with a class discussion that formalizes and solidifies important information and ideas.

Jigsaw allows for differentiation in response to readiness by varying resources based on student language or reading level and assigning topics by complexity. It allows for differentiation by interest by making it possible for students to work in expert groups based on aspects of the topic that are most relevant or appealing to them. Jigsaw working conditions allow for individual as well as collaborative work.

• • •

Some instructional strategies are quite flexible and can address a variety of both content and student needs. For example, learning contracts can help teachers address student readiness, interest, or learning profile, and that can be useful in differentiating content, process, or product. Some other strategies serve a more specialized function. Concept attainment, for instance, is most likely to help teachers address readiness needs for students who do not already have a grasp of the content it introduces. Some instructional strategies—for example, small-group instruction or mini-workshops—are classroom workhorses that require minimal teacher preparation time and can be used often to benefit learning. Others—for example, orbital studies, independent studies, or entry points—lend themselves to occasional use and often necessitate more extended teacher preparation. A goal of the teacher over time should be to develop an extensive tool kit of strategies that facilitate teaching and enhance learning at any point in a learning cycle.

9

How Do Teachers Make It All Work?

Students at work create various kinds of noise. They talk and measure and puzzle out and make the audible messes that an assistant principal is supposed to abhor. Their activity also exposes the inconvenient truth that some kids do the work faster than others. The neat march over material that is possible when only the teacher sets the pace of the journey is no longer possible.

Theodore Sizer, *Horace's School*

To this point, we have focused largely on issues related to differentiating curriculum and instruction and on how assessment and environment can support the success of those two endeavors. The tone, procedures, and processes that constitute classroom management provide a context in which other elements can play out effectively and efficiently—or a context that fetters them and thwarts their potential. If curriculum and instruction are the heart and limbs of sound teaching, then classroom management is the central nervous system. Without the heart, there is no life, but without the nervous system, there is no function. This chapter focuses on classroom management that supports differentiated instruction and is a natural outgrowth of its philosophy.

Images of School

We all have our own images of how to "do" school. Parents base their images on the 13 or more years they spent in school. As teachers, we create different images of school: from our own early schooling through professional training to our first years teaching in the classroom. Students create their images of school, day after day, in their pilgrimage to become "educated."

Cartoons, movies, television, the Internet, and books also fuel images of school. As a rule, these images are dominated by rows of desks and a teacher working in front of the group. Students wait passively—slouched or wiggling—for the teacher to do whatever she had in mind for the day. Few of these images prepare us to envision, let alone craft, classrooms that are differentiated in response to the array of children's learning needs.

Alas, there is no fail-safe way to master approaches to teaching and learning that common sense (and tomes of research) tells us would be more effective with contemporary students. Although this chapter cannot provide all the answers, it offers broad guidelines for those who seek more promising ways of thinking about, planning for, and being leaders in differentiated classrooms.

Getting Started

If the notion of a student-centered, differentiated classroom is new to you, here are a few suggestions to help steer your thinking and planning in that direction. They are, for the most part, practical and concrete—because that's what is needed when beginning something new—but also include some more reflective and long-term suggestions.

Examine Your Philosophy About Individual Needs

A young teacher working hard to implement a differentiated classroom once reflected, "Differentiated instruction isn't a strategy. It's a way of thinking about all you do when you teach and all the kids do when they learn." Not only was she correct, but her insight also offers important guidance. Instead of first focusing on what to do in the classroom to "manage" students, focus on how to think about effective teaching and learning, and then think about ways in which you can "lead" (not "manage") your students in creating a classroom that aims to work for everyone (Tomlinson & Imbeau, 2010). Here are some questions to get you started:

• Which makes more sense to you: that you do most of the work in the classroom or that students be the primary workers and thinkers? Why?

• Does it seem more beneficial to you that everyone should always need the same book, website, math problem, art lesson, or homework? Or are students likely to show up at different points of readiness for reading and math and drawing and everything else we teach in schools? Why do you say so?

• Do students all seem to learn in the same way or at the same pace? Or do some process information differently and at a different pace than others? How do you know?

• Do you learn more about your students by talking *to* them or by talking *with* them? Why?

• Do students become independent learners in classrooms where they are always told what to do? Or do they become independent when teachers systematically give them more responsibility for learning and teach them how to use the independence wisely? Why?

• Do learners care if they have choices about what and how to learn? Do they care a lot or a little? Why is that the case?

• Are we more motivated to grow when we try to reach our own ceilings or when the ceilings are someone else's? Why do you say so?

• In general, are you more effective and efficient at teaching small groups of students and individuals, or are you more effective with the whole class? Why do you say so?

• Is learning richer and more permanent when it's rote or meaning-based? How do you know?

• Are students more likely to work in a setting where they've helped to craft routines and processes or one in which they feel like pieces on a game board, being manipulated by someone else? What's your evidence for your answer?

Add your own questions about teaching to this list; there should be an unlimited supply of them. In the end, your evolving beliefs about your classroom will guide your choices as you plan for and reflect on instruction. Knowing what you believe also will help you feel more comfortable and confident in answering questions from your students, colleagues, administrators, and families about why you teach as you do.

Start Small

Like students, teachers are ready for differing degrees of challenge. Many teachers successfully start differentiating instruction with small, well-orchestrated changes.

Begin the process of differentiation by teaching all of your students to do an "anchor activity," which is meaningful work done individually and silently. This could be journal writing, free reading, foreign language pattern drills, seatwork in math, or sketchbook assignments. It's something useful and important for students to do on a relatively regular basis throughout at least a portion of the year. It may seem a bit of a paradox to begin differentiation by not differentiating. But when you ask all students to learn to work absolutely quietly on one anchor activity (or more), you pave the way for breaking off individuals or small groups to do other tasks while the remaining students continue with the comfortable, predictable anchor activity.

Early on, you may want to ask some students to work on an anchor activity and others to work on a different task that also requires no conversation or collaboration. This introduces the idea that students won't always do the same work. You create an atmosphere that's conducive to individual focus, and you emphasize attending to one's own work rather than focusing on what someone else does.

Then, try a differentiated task for a small block of time. In a primary classroom, for example, begin a language arts period with all students doing paired reading from the same "reading boxes." After 10 minutes of paired reading differentiated by reading readiness, call all students to the reading corner to listen to a story together, then discuss it as a whole class. In a middle school history class, begin with a whole-class discussion and common use of a graphic organizer to compare two time periods. For the last 10 minutes of class, ask students to do one of two entries in their learning logs or personal journals. The entries can be at different levels of complexity or based on two different interest areas.

Starting small like this is the "think-versus-sink" approach: you think your way to success without sinking beneath too many changes. You also teach your students, step by step, to succeed in an independent, learner-centered class. It's not wise to ask them to manage too many routines and processes for which they are unprepared.

Grow Slowly—but Grow

It's better just to do a few things well. Set goals for yourself, and stick with them, but make sure they are reasonable goals. Like students, teachers grow best when they are moderately challenged. Waiting until conditions are ideal or until you are sure of yourself yields lethargy, not growth. On the other hand, trying to do too many things before you have a chance to think them through leads to frustration and failure. Here are some small but significant starts that might work for you. Pick one or two of them as goals for a year.

• Take notes on your students each day—electronically or on paper. Be conscious of what works and what doesn't and for which learners.

• Assess students before you begin to teach a skill or topic. Study the pre-assessment results and their implications for you and your students.

• Think of all work students do (discussions, journal entries, centers, products, quizzes, group tasks, homework) as indicators of student need, not marks in a grade book.

• Create one differentiated lesson per unit.

• Differentiate one product per semester.

• Find multiple resources for a couple of key parts of your curriculum. For example, consider using several textbooks, supplementary books or websites at varied readability levels (from basic to quite advanced), videos, or audiotapes that you or volunteers make over time to support student growth and success with text.

• Establish class criteria for success with tasks or products, then work with students to add personal criteria to their lists. You can add one or two for each child based on what you know of the student's strengths and needs.

• Give students more choices about how to work, how to express learning, or which homework assignments to do. (Generally, structured choices work best at first.)

• Develop and use a two-day learning contract the first marking period, a four-day learning contract the second marking period, and a week-long learning contract the third marking period.

These are just a few possibilities. The idea is to commit to growth. Try something new, reflect on what you learn from the experience, and apply those insights to the next new step.

Envision How an Activity Will Look

Olympic athletes often pause before an event, close their eyes, and see themselves completing the competition. They visualize clearing the vault, making the ski jump, or completing the dive. This is a good idea for a teacher in a differentiated classroom, too.

Take time before the day begins to ask yourself how you want a differentiated activity to begin, what you want it to look like as it progresses, and how it should end. Think about what could go wrong along the way, and plan to keep those things from happening. Write out procedures for yourself and directions you'll give students. Of course you can't envision every possible snag, but you'll get better and better at second-guessing and at making plans and giving successful directions. Especially in the early stages, improvisational differentiation is less likely to succeed than choreographed differentiation.

Step Back and Reflect

As you work your way into a differentiated classroom, be sure you think your way into it as well. When you try something new, take time to reflect before you take the next step. You might ask yourself these questions:

• Which students seemed to be engaged in learning? Which were not? Do you know why?

• What evidence do you have that each student understood or "owned" what you hoped would come from the lesson? Do you need to get more evidence to answer this question?

• How did you feel about your introduction to the activity or lesson?

• In what ways did the activity or lesson begin as you wished? Did it get off track? How? What worked and what didn't as students began to work? Were your directions clear? Were materials easily accessible? Did you specify the time for moving (to stations, centers, or small groups)? Did you specify and reinforce the time allotted to settle down?

• As the activity or lesson progressed, how well did students remain focused? If there was a point where focus was ragged, can you figure out why? If everyone maintained focus throughout, why did things work so well? How did group size work? Do any students need to sit in a different place in the room? Did you see any pairings or groups that were unproductive? Were there students who did not work well in groups or did not work well alone? Did students know how to monitor their work? Did they know how to get help?

• How was the conclusion to the activity or lesson? Was there enough warning for students to stop their work in an organized way? Did they know where to put materials and supplies? Were a few students specified to put away materials, move furniture, or handle other clean-up tasks? Were things well organized for the next class or the next day? Did students make the transition to the next class or next activity in a self-controlled way?

• Did you have a sense of who was learning what as the lesson progressed? How did you interact with individuals and groups as they worked? What useful information did you gather as you moved among groups? What effective coaching were you able to do? How might you improve your data gathering and coaching?

Make notes of things you want to retain the next time you try a differentiated activity and things you want to improve. Make specific plans to use the insights you gain from your reflection.

Settling In for the Long Haul

If your teaching philosophy embraces attention to individual students, and if you develop routines and procedures for a differentiated classroom in a systematic and reflective way, differentiation gradually will become a way of life. It won't be something you do every once in a great while. At that point, you need to incorporate at least three things into your routines.

Talk with Students Early and Often

As you develop a clear philosophy about what it means to differentiate instruction, share your thinking with your students. Be a metacognitive teacher: unpack your thinking in conversations with students. Compared to the images many students have about school, you're changing the "rules." Let them know why and how. Here are some ideas that may help you involve your students in creating a responsive classroom.

Use an activity that helps students reflect on the fact that they differ from one another in how they learn and what they like to learn about. (They already know this fact quite clearly, by the way.) Depending on students' ages, the activity will vary. Some teachers ask their students to graph their strengths and weaknesses on a range of skills related and unrelated to the class in question. Some teachers have their students write autobiographies about themselves as learners. Some ask students to search for images on the Internet that represent their own school experiences and to explain why they chose the image they did.

For example, a teacher of young children sent home a survey asking families to provide the ages at which the children sat up, walked, ran, talked, got their first tooth, lost their first tooth, and rode a bike. She helped students create bar graphs that showed how children do things on different timetables. The class concluded *when* we learn to talk isn't nearly as important as *that* we learn to talk. Throughout the year, she brought students back to the graphs to remind them it was fine if some students learned a skill before or after others. In the end, what mattered was learning the skill and using it well.

Whatever the approach, reflect on student questions and comments about positive and negative school experiences, best and worst subjects, and effective and ineffective ways of learning.

Let students know that their differing strengths, needs, and learning preferences present an interesting challenge to you as a teacher. Ask them whether or not they believe you should pay attention to developing their individual strengths and helping them improve in difficult areas by focusing on the ways that work best for them individually. Or do they believe you will do a better job of teaching by ignoring those things and doing the same thing for everyone all the time? Chances are, they won't choose the "forget-who-we-are" approach.

Begin an ongoing discussion of how a differentiated classroom looks and operates. Talk about how your role will differ. For example, you'll work with small groups and individuals rather than only the whole class. Students' roles will differ, too: they'll help and support one another's learning in different ways, making it possible for you to work with individuals and small groups. Students will take more responsibility for class operation, using time wisely so everyone can learn. Their assignments will differ, too; not everyone will always have the same assignment in class or for homework. The classroom will look different, with small groups or individuals working on various tasks. Students will see more movement, and they'll use a wider range of materials.

Ask students to help you establish guidelines and procedures to make the classroom work. Let them help you decide how to begin class, how to give directions when multiple things are about to begin simultaneously, how they should get help when you are busy, what they must do when they finish an assignment, how to keep the class focused as activities progress, and how to conclude an activity smoothly. These conversations can occur as the need for each procedure emerges, but they are pivotal in establishing and maintaining a successful learning environment.

Continue to Empower Students

There will always be classroom roles only the teacher can fulfill. However, many teachers have found it easier to do things for students than to teach them to do those things for themselves. Look for things you don't have to do in the classroom, and gradually prepare your students to do them effectively. For example, can students learn to move furniture efficiently and quietly when the room needs to be rearranged? Can students hand out or collect work folders or other materials? Can students check one another's work in a responsible and helpful way at some points in a learning cycle? Can students learn to straighten up the room? Can they learn to file their own work in designated places rather than bring it to you? Can they learn to keep accurate records of what they complete and when? Can they keep records of their grades to gauge how their performance is progressing? Can they learn to set personal learning goals and to assess their progress according to those goals? The answer to all those questions, and many more like them, is yes—as long as you teach them how! Helping students master these things develops more independent and thoughtful learners, and it also creates a classroom that belongs to kids as much as to adults.

Continue to Be Analytical

Classrooms are busy places. Teachers often get caught in the undertow of "doing" and fail to take time for reflecting. Learning to facilitate a differentiated classroom is like learning to conduct a large orchestra. It calls for many players, many parts, many instruments, and many skills. Skilled conductors hear and see many things at once but also take time away from the podium to reflect on things like the intent of the composer and balance among the sections. They listen to recordings of rehearsals and compare those to performance goals. They identify whether there is a need for additional attention to particular passages or a need for sectional rehearsals.

As your differentiated classroom evolves, cultivate your analytical skills. Some days, just look at how students get into and out of groups, or look only at students who are currently advanced in the subject. Take notes on who elects to work with visual materials and who gravitates to moving around or using ideas in context when given a choice. Tape the class every once in a while, or ask a colleague to be a second pair of eyes in your classroom. In either case, you'll identify things that are going well that you'd have missed otherwise, and you'll discover areas that need additional work.

Be analytical with your students, too. Ask them to recall the guidelines you established together for working effectively in a group. Have them analyze with you procedures that are working well for them and those that are not. Let them make suggestions for how to get even better at working together (or beginning class or moving around the room). Express your pleasure when you see them growing in responsibility and independence. Let them tell you when they feel proud. Work together when there is dissonance, too—not to eliminate the passage from the piece but to attend to it as a whole or in "sectional rehearsals."

Some Practical Considerations

Many years ago, a professor suggested to me that the majority of teaching success stemmed from knowing where to keep the pencils. At the time, I was too much of a novice to know what he was saying, and I thought him shallow. Four decades and thousands of students later, I understand. Here are some mundane but altogether essential hints for your consideration as you establish a differentiated classroom. The list is not exhaustive, and some items will not apply to your classroom, but the thoughts below may prompt you to consider something crucial about "where to put the pencils" in your professional world.

Give Thoughtful Directions

When you give directions for multiple tasks simultaneously, don't give everyone directions for all the tasks. It wastes time, it's confusing, and it calls too much attention to task variance. The trick is how to let everyone know what to do without giving whole-group directions. Try this:

• Start the class with a familiar task. Once students settle in, meet with one small group at a time to give directions for differentiated tasks.

• Give directions today for tomorrow. That is, today, give directions to a careful listener and a careful follower in each group. They can give directions to their group when the task begins tomorrow.

• Use task cards, or put directions on PowerPoint slides, a flip chart, or the whiteboard. Students can go to assigned (or selected) spots in the room and find out what to do by reading a carefully written task card or watching an engaging presentation. With younger students, assign more fluent readers to read task cards to the group at the start of the activity and direct more computer-savvy students to use the whiteboard.

• Use recorded directions. Recorded directions work wonderfully for students who have difficulty with print or with the language of the classroom, when you don't have time to write a task card, or when directions are complex enough you'd like to explain them a couple of ways.

• Think twice about introducing a completely new format in a small-group task. For example, it makes better sense to use graphic organizers several times with the whole class before you ask a small group to use them. Have all students work at the same learning center until they understand how to work there before differentiating work at the center.

• Make yourself "off limits" at strategic times in the instructional sequence. You may want to make it standard procedure that no one can ask you questions during the first five minutes of any activity. That way, you can walk among students, making sure they settle down and have their materials; being cornered by one student may result in others remaining off task. You also need uninterrupted time for meeting with small groups and individuals. With older students, you can just announce those times. With younger ones, you could indicate you're off limits by wearing a ribbon around your neck or a baseball cap. In either case, make certain students understand why they cannot come to you at those times.

Establish Routines for Getting Help

For a variety of reasons, students in a multitask classroom must learn to get help from someone other than you much of the time. Teach them how to do that, and make provisions for help from other sources. Here are some guidelines:

• Work with students on being good listeners. Kids often learn sloppy listening habits because they know someone will reiterate what they miss. Help them learn to focus on you when you talk, ask them to "replay" what you said in their heads, and ask someone to summarize aloud essential directions. They'll learn to need less help if they listen to you well in the first place. This takes time on their part and perseverance on yours.

• Teach students strategies to use if they are stuck about what to do next. The mnemonic RICE (Recall, Imagine, Check, Expert) is an example of a strategy students can use independently. First, they should try hard to recall what you said. If that doesn't work, they should close their eyes, see you talking, use good practical intelligence, and imagine (logically) what the directions would have been for the task. If that doesn't help, they can check with a classmate (someone at their table or nearby doing the same task); this should be done in a whisper. If there's still no sense of direction, they can ask one or more designated "experts of the day" who have the independence or skills necessary to provide guidance. "Experts" should stop their own work only long enough to help someone who is genuinely stuck. (Over time, most students can serve as an expert of the day for one or more tasks.)

• Ensure that students *know* what to do next. In the rare instances where the procedure for getting help fails, students should move on to a preapproved anchor activity. Let them know it's acceptable to tell you how they tried the procedure, came up empty, and began working with the preapproved alternative until they could get your help. It is not acceptable to sit and wait, and it is not acceptable to hinder others.

Always be sure students know how much you value time. Help them understand that there are many important things to accomplish and too little time for doing them. Wise use of time should be a classroom ethic.

Stay Aware, Stay Organized

Many teachers fear that they will not know what's going on when students work with a variety of tasks in a differentiated classroom. An effective teacher can't afford to be "out of the loop." In a differentiated classroom, the teacher should have more awareness of what and how students are doing, not less. Teachers must look at the issue of staying on top of student progress in a different way. Here are some guidelines for keeping yourself organized in order to facilitate students' independent, differentiated work:

• Use student work folders. These always stay in the classroom and contain all work in progress (including partially completed tasks, independent study work, and anchor options). The folders also should contain a record-keeping sheet where students can document work they have completed and date of completion, goals they have met, and individual conferences they've had with you about progress and goals. Older students can keep a running record of grades on the inside cover. Such folders provide you a ready way to review student progress and also can be useful for parent–teacher conferences and conferences among parents, teachers, and students.

• Make a list of all skills and competencies you want your students to master in each facet of your subject (e.g., writing, spelling, comprehension and grammar, computation, problem solving, mathematical reasoning). Then extend the list to skills more basic than the ones you're working toward and skills more advanced than the targeted ones. Turn this into a paper or electronic checklist, with the competencies listed sequentially and a way to record dates and comments for each competency. Make a checklist for each student, and keep the lists alphabetically in a notebook or a computer folder. Periodically spot-check students' work using the checklist, or do a formal written or oral assessment with individuals or the group from time to time. As you record observations over time, you should see a clear pattern of individual growth. This will help you monitor student progress, and it also should be a great help in developing differentiated assignments targeted to student need. These observations aid in student–teacher planning conferences, too.

• Establish carefully organized and coded places where students should place completed assignments (e.g., stack trays, boxes, folders, or electronic files). This is much more effective than having assignments brought to you, and it is more effective than having a variety of assignments all piled together.

• Carry a clipboard or an electronic tablet around the class with you. Make brief notes about nifty things you see students do, "aha" moments, points of confusion, or working conditions that need to be tightened. Use the notes for reflection, planning, and individual and classroom conversations.

Don't feel compelled to grade everything. (You'd never think of grading a piano student's every practice session!) There's a time for students to figure things out and a time for judging whether they did, but the two shouldn't always be the same. Help your students see how important it is to complete activities so they become more and more skilled and insightful. Use peer checkers or "experts of the day" when an accuracy check is necessary. Provide focused feedback regularly and help students learn to do the same for one another. When it's time for formal assessment, help students see the link between good practice and success.

When students are working with sense-making activities and you feel compelled to grade, focus on things like whether the student stayed on task, worked hard, got help appropriately, revised work to improve its quality, and moved to anchor activities when work was completed. On your clipboard or tablet, you might keep a class list with spaces for a daily assessment of these sorts of things. If you see a student have a breakthrough or make a real leap of progress, put a plus in today's space. If a student has real difficulty staying on task despite reminders, put a minus in today's space. Later, put checks in the other spaces indicating that the student was working appropriately. Look for patterns over time, and work with what they tell you. Although you could convert the pattern into a single "daily work" grade if necessary, there are plenty of other opportunities for formal grading. Use the patterns you see to help students be more reflective about their own habits of mind and work. Remember that continual grading impairs students' willingness to make and learn from mistakes, makes them teacher-dependent, and teaches them to learn for grades, not for its own value (Earl, 2003; O'Connor, 2011; Tomlinson & Moon, 2013). All this grading also makes you crazy and robs you of important thinking and planning time.

Consider "Home Base" Seats

In a differentiated classroom, it's often helpful to have students assigned to "home base" seats where they begin and end class every day. Students always begin the class at "home base," and some days they remain there. When differentiated activities lead them to other parts of the room, they return to home base when the class ends.

Using home base seats helps you check attendance quickly and makes it simple for students to distribute work folders for you. It makes it easier to ensure that the room is straight at the end of an activity and provides an orderly format for dismissal or transition. Assigned seats also let you develop positive peer groupings for those times when students work at home base.

Establish Start-Up and Wrap-Up Procedures

Before students begin to move to various work areas, let them know how quickly they should be in their new places and working. You should make the time realistic but also a bit on the stingy side. After students move through the room, let them know how they did. Work with them so they get used to settling in efficiently.

During the activity, keep your eye on the clock. Give students a two-minute signal that their work time is about to end (flash the lights or just walk to each table and tell them). Follow that with another signal to return to home-base seating. Students should know that you expect them to return to those seats within 30 seconds, in an orderly and quiet way.

Teach Students to Work for Quality

A few students in every class seem inclined to measure their success by how quickly they complete their work rather than by how thoughtful they are in doing it. Be clear with your students that craftsmanship and a sense of pride in work are what matter. Help them understand why by asking them to analyze the differences in work that is hastily finished versus work that shows persistence, revision, and creativity.

Sometimes, students finish work quickly because it's too easy for them or the directions don't clearly state standards of excellence. When those are not problems, patiently and persistently insist that only quality work is acceptable. One teacher called it "working for a Bingo." She taught her students to resist the urge to turn in work until they had done absolutely everything they could think of to improve it. Then they could say, "Bingo! That's it! That's my very best."

Preempt Challenging Behavior

Students whose behavior both challenges the teacher and damps the student's success can also discourage a teacher from establishing classroom routines that call for students to function thoughtfully and with respect for themselves and others. There are many reasons why students "challenge the system," and there is surely no way to generalize a single solution for helping those students gradually but steadily assume responsibility for their own learning. In many ways, these students, even more than their more focused classmates, need what a differentiated classroom offers: belief in their capacity to succeed, support for that success, a measured and stepwise plan for helping students move ahead from their points of entry, meaning-rich curriculum, a range of ways to learn and express learning, and classroom routines that balance structure and flexibility.

Such students often respond well to teachers who are "warm demanders" (Bondy & Ross, 2008). These teachers convey a strong sense of trust and acceptance but simultaneously make clear that they expect only the best from their students. Warm demanders consistently provide the structure, explanation, and scaffolding that support students' best efforts and do so in a way that is rooted in caring. They don't give up on students, compromise their expectations, or dilute their instruction in the face of challenging behavior. Rather, they coach the student to play a better game. Virtually all students can grow in autonomy and are more likely to do so in the context of a classroom that respects that reality.

Developing a Support System

At least four groups can help you on your path to a differentiated classroom. Colleagues, administrators, parents, and community members all can aid you and your students. With all four groups, however, you'll probably have to take the initiative to enlist their help.

Calling on Colleagues

The unhappy truth in many schools is that some of your colleagues will be resentful if you do something innovative or expend more energy in your work than is the norm. A happier truth is that, in these same settings, there are always a few soul mates who are energized by their work, catalyzed by someone else's ideas, and ready to take the risk of growth. Find one or two people from this group and work with them.

In many schools, an art teacher, a special educator, a teacher of the gifted, and a few classroom teachers already differentiate instruction. They may not feel like experts, but neither do you. They have great ideas and routines already in place; you have ideas and questions that can enrich their work. At the very least, they'll feel complimented by your wanting to learn from and with them. Meet with them regularly, arrange to spend time in one another's classrooms, plan together, troubleshoot as a team, share lessons and materials, and take turns teaching and watching as peer coaches. The synergy from such collegial partnerships can be one of the most amazing benefits of a job that all too often is isolating.

Making Principals Partners

Some principals are suspicious of movement and talking in a classroom. I once watched a colleague with whom I was team teaching change such an attitude. She was clear in her own mind about what we were doing in our differentiated classroom and why it was important. She often stopped by the principal's office to say, "When you're out and about in the halls today, you'll notice our students are working in groups." She'd explain why and add, "I hope you'll stop by and take a look." In the beginning, that's what the principal did. He would pause beside the door briefly. When he eventually accepted her invitation to "step in and watch a while," she encouraged him to talk with the students to satisfy himself that they knew what they were doing. While we were teaching our students to be resourceful and independent, she was teaching the principal to appreciate that sort of classroom. He became our biggest champion. If your principal is suspicious of differentiation, or not supportive for some other reason, try being his or her teacher, too!

If your building administrator already supports student-centered, differentiated classrooms, share your personal goals for the month or the year. Invite your principal to help you figure out how to achieve those goals in your classroom. Your principal then can target observations more appropriately, and you can draw on the insights of a veteran educator who sees lots of classrooms in action.

Bringing Parents Aboard

Clearly, most parents want good things for their children in school. They want their children to grow, to maximize their strengths and minimize their weaknesses, to find the classroom exciting, and to wake up eager to go to school the next morning. Yet as surely as a differentiated classroom must confront children's images of how we "do" school, it also must deal with parents' stereotypical images of school.

At the beginning of the school year, send an e-mail or a note home asking parents to tell you their hopes for the coming year in school. Really listen and learn. Systematically show parents how a differentiated classroom acknowledges and builds on children's strengths, provides opportunities to bolster weaker areas, keeps track of individual growth, and promotes engagement and excitement. Use periodic e-mails, the class website, parent–teacher conferences focused on reviewing student work, and students' own self-evaluations to help parents understand how your curriculum and way of instruction reflect the same goals they have for their youngsters.

You might even invite parents to take an active role in the class. Volunteers can review math concepts with struggling learners, read with advanced readers who can benefit from conversations about reading, or work on projects with students—sending the message that adults find them worthy of time and attention. Parents also can be a treasure trove of novels, computer expertise, maps, or hands-on learning materials—all things that expand the learning options for their own and others' children.

Home–school partnerships are important to differentiated classrooms. Parents always know their children more deeply than a teacher possibly can. There's much for the teacher to learn from that depth of knowledge. On the other hand, a teacher knows a child in other ways, and parents gain from that breadth of knowledge. Looking at a child from both of these viewpoints increases the chances of helping that child realize his or her full potential. The wisest teachers teach parents as well as children, and they eagerly seek opportunities to learn from parents as well.

Involving the Community

The world outside the classroom offers more opportunities than even the most magical classroom. It makes sense to open up a differentiated classroom to that larger world. Frederick learns best when he builds models of things. Phan needs someone to toss around ideas in his native language before he writes in English. Saranne is more advanced in computers than any adult in her building, and 4th grader Charlie has pretty well finished 6th grade math. Francie desperately wants to know how to dance, Philip is itchy to learn about archaeology, and Genice wants to use a digital camera and video animation to do her history project. The teacher who can facilitate all those things is rare indeed.

However, service clubs can make recordings of text for struggling readers and students with learning disabilities, and many textbook companies now commonly offer audio and digital versions of their materials. Mentors can help students discover a world of possibilities with photography, baseball statistics, computer animation, or jazz. A church can provide volunteers for students trying to communicate in two languages. A company can provide old carpet squares to cover a reading corner in the classroom. Museums and galleries can provide ideas, materials, guidance on independent projects, virtual field trips, and access to online collections. A senior citizens' center can provide guidance and resources for a wide range of orbital investigations (see Chapter 7). The world is a classroom replete with resources and mentors. A generous teacher links learners with those wide options.

●   ●   ●

Again, you don't need to try to do everything at once. Each year, devise one new way to link up with a colleague, gain insight and support from an administrator, learn from and teach parents, or invite a bit of the world into your classroom. Remember that becoming an expert at differentiation is a career-long goal. One step at a time, you will get there.

10

Education Leaders as Catalysts for Differentiated Classrooms

It is so easy to underestimate the complexities of the change process. . . . Change is difficult because it is riddled with dilemmas, ambivalences, and paradoxes. It combines steps that do not seem to go together: to have a clear vision and be open-minded; to take initiative and empower others; to provide support and pressure; to start small and think big; to expect results and be patient and persistent; to have a plan and be flexible; to use top-down and bottom-up strategies; to experience uncertainty and satisfaction.

Michael G. Fullan and Suzanne Stiegelbauer,
The New Meaning of Educational Change

Differentiation is not an instructional strategy, a collection of strategies, or a teaching model. It's a way of thinking about teaching and learning that advocates beginning where individuals are rather than with a prescribed plan of action that ignores student variance. It is a way of thinking that challenges how educators typically envision assessment, teaching, learning, classroom roles, use of time, and curriculum. It is also a way of thinking that stems from our best understanding of how people learn.

Individual teachers who feel a need to take up this challenge will read books like this one, meld its philosophies with their practice, and reshape their classrooms. Often, however, growth-focused education leaders see a need for change on a broader scale.

This chapter is directed toward department chairs, principals, district-level administrators, and others in leadership positions who want to be catalysts for developing differentiated classrooms. Although school change is difficult, it is not out of reach, and it is more likely to occur if it is grounded in the best current knowledge of the change process. This is a vital understanding, because schools embark on a path of significant change when they begin to develop differentiated classrooms.

Experience, Research, and School Change

We know much about the change process in education: what supports and undermines it, its stages, and the roles and responses of various participants. The scope of this chapter is not adequate even to summarize the work of researchers like Michael Fullan (1993, 2001a, 2001b), Seymour Sarason (e.g., 1990, 1993), Robert Evans (1996), Thomas Sergiovanni (e.g., 1999, 2005), and others whose insights have illuminated a murky process. Nonetheless, key conclusions from their work support the advice in the section to come: some essential principles for guiding change in schools. This is not meant to be linear advice; change is complex, messy, and unpredictable. When we undertake change, we start, we start over, and we even skip steps. Yet all of the following suggestions are important for reflection, over time, as a school or district leader guides change leading to differentiated classrooms.

Examine Your Beliefs and Goals

Spend time thinking about why the idea of differentiated classrooms is sensible and important to you. Is it because you believe profoundly in the importance of effective heterogeneous communities of learning for the future of schools and society? Is it because you see too many students disenchanted with standardized classes? Is it because of what you know about cognitive psychology and how the brain works? Is it because you want to save money? Not all motivations are equal.

You must know why you think it's worth the trouble to create differentiated classes. You must be able to articulate your viewpoint clearly and believably to those you lead. If you do not have a compelling sense of why differentiated classrooms are worthwhile, you would be wise to move away from differentiation as a focus of your leadership.

Establish and Share a Vision

Leadership has a great deal to do with creating a vision and inspiring others to join you in working to achieve it. What might classrooms in your school or district look like if change occurs? Why would that be positive? For whom?

Don't ask teachers to do something shrouded in uncertainty. Be sure you are clear on your definition of and goals for differentiation. Explain these so others can examine them and talk with you about them. Then do a difficult thing: hold the vision with one hand and reach out with the other to invite other leaders, teachers, and parents to revise and extend that vision. It is a paradox of change that leaders must believe in their ideas but be open to the reality that others will necessarily reshape those ideas in positive ways for change to truly happen.

The goal is clear: you want to foster classrooms where excellent teaching is targeted to the variable learning needs of diverse students. This book offers one way to think about reaching that goal. There are other ways to think about it. Remain open to all ideas, and invite other stakeholders to help you think more broadly. Initiating change begins with sharing a sense of direction, but you also must understand that few worthwhile journeys progress in a straight line.

Avoid Overload

Teachers often perceive that they are asked to learn about and implement multiple disconnected initiatives simultaneously. They will rightfully feel discouraged or angry if they sense that differentiating instruction is just one more thing they are expected to do. To that end, it's vital to avoid a feeling of overload among teachers.

To plant the seeds for effective change, leaders first need to focus on one key goal, such as making classrooms more responsive to the full range of learners. Ensure that the goal remains central in everyone's thinking. As much as possible, defer initiatives that impede attention to that goal and present initiatives that help achieve the goal in that context. For example, say to faculty, "We are learning about literature circles because they help us attend to differences in student readiness and interests in the following ways." Or explain that learning about cultural and gender patterns "can help us achieve our goals of responsive classrooms in the following ways." Or demonstrate: "By using these apps in these ways, we will be able to address the learning needs of many of our students more effectively." In other words, as often as possible, the message should be, "We're doing what our diverse students need us to do to maximize their learning. What we're talking about today will help us achieve this goal."

Prepare for the Long Haul

Substantial change is a slow process that must be initiated, implemented, and institutionalized. It almost inevitably requires 5 to 10 years for significant change to develop sturdy "roots." If you are serious about crafting differentiated classrooms, make a time line and plan of that duration. Let others know the idea is "here to stay" by publishing essentials of the plan and time line so they can take the long look with you. Of course, the plan will be reshaped over time, and the time line will be revised. But you should demonstrate an unshakable commitment to the duration required to make meaningful change.

Education leaders have a destructive habit of ballyhooing the fad of the year, or even of the month, and then backing off. Many teachers know that if they lie low for a while, the pesky initiative they'd like to avoid will vanish. There is no quick fix to making differentiation a reality. Setting a one-year goal dooms the idea to failure, and it diminishes the chance that your colleagues will ever really learn to do what is required for meaningful change in their classrooms.

Start Smart

To start smart, first begin small. Try a few pilot teachers and classrooms rather than a whole school or a whole district. But do start, and start with full support to make sure observable changes occur in classroom practice early in the process. Begin with teachers who have the skill and will to change. These teachers are already reflective about their practice, sensitive to their students, flexible in their instructional patterns, and ready to learn. This will yield early successes, strategies for dealing with inevitable problems, and a cadre of teachers who can become staff developers as the process expands. Then, create teams of teachers who can work together, share ideas and materials, troubleshoot with one another, co-teach, or observe one another and provide feedback. Collegiality, not isolation, is far more nourishing to new ideas.

Once you have established this core group, go for action and beliefs. It's extremely important for teachers to think about their beliefs as change occurs. For example, implementing a new approach to teaching math without a sense of how it fits into the larger picture of learning is likely to result in an ill-used strategy. On the other hand, teaching makes pragmatists of teachers. They are more likely to change their beliefs because of something they successfully implement in their classrooms; they won't necessarily try a new approach just because they have changed their beliefs. Be sure you help teachers identify something they will actually do in their classrooms, while continuing the conversation about why a particular action matters and how it works to support student growth.

Model the Process of Differentiation

In a differentiated classroom, a teacher says something like this to students:

> Here's where we're headed. That we all learn and grow and work hard in the process is not negotiable; how we reach the destination is. Some of us may move more rapidly than others. Some begin further ahead. Some may succeed better with Plan A, others with Plan B. Sometimes I, as teacher, will make some decisions. Sometimes you, as students, will make them. Often, we will make them together. We will always try to make them in ways that help us all achieve the goal of maximum growth.

When education leaders begin an initiative like differentiated instruction, they take on the teacher role. Schools and teachers differ. That they all make progress toward the goal of differentiated classrooms is not negotiable. How they get there is. Different schools and various teachers have differing readiness levels, interests, and learning profiles. They will need to develop the process of differentiation on different timetables, through different routes, and with differing forms of assistance. Sometimes leaders will make key decisions. Sometimes teachers must make them. Often, they need to be made jointly—and always with an eye to maximizing progress toward differentiated classrooms. Leaders who model differentiation exemplify the kind of respectful environment needed in responsive classrooms. Leaders and models also provide natural opportunities to talk with colleagues about how differentiation works.

Examine Policies and Procedures

Often, leaders ask teachers to accomplish objectives even though national, state, district, and local policies and procedures make it difficult to do so. Sometimes leaders will need to work with colleagues to modify competing mandates or processes in order to open the way to addressing learners' varying needs. Here are some questions to consider:

• Can you adjust school schedules to provide teachers larger blocks of uninterrupted instructional time? It is difficult to set up and carry out a differentiated science lab in a 40-minute class period.

• Should your district consider adopting multiple texts rather than one text for a given subject and grade level? A district that mandates using the same books for all 3rd graders sends a message that differentiation may not be so important.

• Should your district consider modified report cards that include data on students' habits of mind and work and personal growth rather than focusing only on academic performance?

• Should your school consider narrowing the range of learners in some classrooms? Teaching in Noah's Ark, with two of every kind of learner in the school population, may not be the most encouraging or efficient early approach to student assignment for all teachers. Although homogeneous grouping is not a good solution for establishing equitable communities of learning, in the early stages of differentiation, some teachers may be over-extended by trying to address every sort of learning need in one classroom.

• What ways can you find to reduce class size, find more helpers, or increase classroom space or planning time for teachers willing to significantly differentiate instruction (at least in the early stages of teacher learning)?

• Do you need to communicate with parents about differentiation from a school or district level? Or do you expect teachers alone to educate parents about the approach, its potential benefits to students, and opportunities for participation?

Sometimes leaders can't change things; they only can help teachers rethink particular policies or procedures. For example, many teachers see the emphasis on standardized testing as contradictory to attending to student differences. Actually, dragging all students through the same material whether they are academically advanced or feel hopelessly behind, at a speed that is unrealistically fast for most and too slow for some, and in the same teacher-focused mode has never yielded a set of ideal scores. It certainly has never generated a group of stimulated and excited learners. Effective differentiation makes it possible for more students to do better on standardized measures. Leaders can help teachers realize there is no paradox involved in effective teaching.

Top-down standards and curriculum guides should never "become" the curriculum. They can, however, be incorporated into instructional planning that engages students. Helping teachers see the difference, and giving them the freedom to take the more engaging approach, is essential to making differentiated classrooms a reality. A district-level leader whose words and actions convey the message that teachers' success and worth depend on their capacity to get everyone to score "above average" on a particular test given on a specified day of the year should not simultaneously mandate differentiated classrooms.

Plan Staff Development for the Complexity of Change

Early in the process of change, it is useful to have staff development sessions where differentiation is defined, discussed, and illustrated. If such sessions are a match with school or district definitions, principles, and goals—and if they are convincingly presented—they can be a part of effective orientation to an idea. Continued "frontal" presentations, however, rapidly lose their power to generate action.

There is a time when teachers need new information about a topic: its concepts, principles, and skills. This may be accomplished through staff development presentations, reading, watching videos, or individual and small-group inquiry. Then teachers need time and opportunity to make sense of the new ideas; leaders must provide time and structures that promote teacher reflection on the ideas. Teachers need to be able to set long-term and short-term personal goals for translating the ideas into classroom action and to make specific plans for implementation. To support teachers in this process, first encourage them to plan in pairs, and then arrange for co-teaching, peer observation, and peer debriefing.

At that point, based on what they have learned from the translation attempt (including self-reflection, peer input, and student feedback), teachers may be ready for additional information, help with polishing the skills they have attempted, or exposure to another procedure, with additional responsive input.

The staff development cycle is much like good teaching in the classroom. Staff developers must

• Know essential facts, concepts, principles, and skills necessary to attain desired outcomes;

• Develop a sequence of presenting them or having the learners encounter them;

• Assess learner readiness for mastering them;

• Provide opportunities for learners to make sense of and try out the new ideas;

• Provide focused feedback on the learner's application of the ideas; and

• Tailor the next learning opportunity to the learner's current needs.

Keep in mind the various continuums on which learners differ. Some teachers may have the skill to conceive sound differentiated instruction but lack the will to do so. Some may have the will but lack the skill to think about their curriculum in a new way. Some can handle a new approach to curriculum but stumble when it comes to setting up a student-centered classroom. Others already may have a student-centered classroom but find it difficult to work with an understanding- or meaning-based approach to teaching. Some, but not all, will need guidance in developing a new belief system. One-size-fits-all staff development is wrong for work on differentiated classrooms. Staff development is another important opportunity to model what you believe.

Provide Ongoing Assistance

Throughout the long change cycle, teachers will need sustained support. They need leaders to help them by

• Clarifying objectives for teacher growth;

• Giving them time to plan differentiated lessons;

• Creating differentiated curricula when curriculum guides are revised;

• Providing opportunities to visit differentiated classrooms;

• Giving access to a wide range of learner-focused technologies and materials;

• Making it safe to try a new approach in the classroom, with no fear of judgment if there is noise or clutter for a while;

• Giving meaningful, targeted feedback on differentiation work;

• Providing networks of mutual support and encouragement for teachers who are early subscribers to the initiative so they do not feel alone if they are "punished" by colleagues who resist the change; and

• Expressing clear appreciation when they have done a good job or have taken a risk that was less than successful.

Effective leaders continue to look for ways to support and sustain teacher efforts. They do not send teachers alone into uncharted territory.

Apply Pressure and Offer Support

Teaching as it is often practiced invites inertia. So many students have so many needs and require so many teacher interactions each day. Much about schools and classrooms makes it easy to resist change, to wait for a "better" day to try differentiating instruction.

I once heard a speaker say that teachers change either because they see the light or because they feel the heat. Both are motivators; effective administrators must be sources of both light and heat, helping teachers see the benefits of new initiatives while simultaneously insisting on progress. Teacher leaders such as subject-area coordinators, grade-level chairs, and special education teachers are good sources of light, but generally they have no capacity to apply heat. They should not feel ineffective because of this. Instead, teacher leaders must be supported with heat from those whose positions allow them to generate it.

Link Differentiation to Professional Responsibility

Although the term *differentiating instruction* may be relatively new, the idea of tailoring a service to meet a client's needs is not. Even in education, where clients arrive in batches of 20 to 30 at a time, teachers learn early that individuals are not alike and do not "get" what's presented in lockstep fashion. Although many teachers do not practice proactive differentiation based on ongoing assessment and preplanned to target a range of needs, most do believe that it is the teacher's role to help each student succeed.

Helping teachers develop an understanding of their professional responsibility to engage every student in meaningful and powerful learning is at the core of moving toward differentiated classrooms. Charlotte Danielson's (2007) framework for thinking about teacher development in four key domains of teaching (i.e., planning and preparation, classroom environment, instruction, professional responsibilities) proposes standards and benchmarks at levels of performance she calls *unsatisfactory*, *basic*, *proficient*, and *distinguished*.

Throughout Danielson's rich and extensive framework, distinguished performance is marked by responsiveness to students' varying needs. This framework is not intended to overlay differentiated instruction; rather, it reflects the reality that a hallmark of excellent teachers is their capacity to see and serve individuals rather than batches of children.

Using a framework such as Danielson's can help teachers grow in competence and confidence in reaching individual learners, by encouraging reflection on and refining of their efforts. Such benchmarks are particularly helpful when they are part of a teacher assessment process through which teachers set personal goals for responsive teaching, take action toward those goals, receive targeted feedback from leaders who effectively support their progress, and have access to quality professional development to sustain their growth over time. Such an approach should be a source of both light and heat by providing insight about implementation and accountability.

A more detailed illustration of the connections between the Danielson framework and differentiated instruction—one that highlights how differentiation can be considered a professional responsibility—is available online at the ASCD website (www.ascd.org/ASCD/pdf/books/TDC14.pdf).

A Word About Novice Teachers

The quality of tomorrow's classrooms rests squarely on how we are preparing the next generation of teachers today. Research suggests that teacher education programs too often fall short in preparing preservice teachers for the inevitability of academically diverse classrooms (Santangelo & Tomlinson, 2009; Tomlinson et al., 1997). For example, preservice teachers

• Seldom, if ever, experience differentiated instruction in their teacher preparation programs;

• Generally have only one survey course about exceptional children to help them understand the needs of academically diverse learners and, almost without exception, report that this class dealt exclusively with learner traits, offering little guidance in "what to do with them";

• Are rarely encouraged to actively differentiate instruction by education professors, university supervisors, or master teachers;

• Are often discouraged from differentiation, particularly by master teachers who encourage them to "keep everyone together";

• Have few instructional strategies with which they feel comfortable and thus have a shallow well of options for addressing diverse needs; and

• Have few, if any, images of multitasking classrooms to carry with them into their first teaching assignments.

Once in their own classrooms, the undertow for new teachers to "teach to the middle" is profound, both because of the complexity of teaching and because of peer pressure to conform to "the way we do school here." Novice teachers who have a strong, consistent emphasis on differentiation in their teacher education programs and master teachers who differentiate instruction are far more likely to attempt to address varied learner needs in their early teaching.

Early teaching is a time to develop the "gross motor skills" of the profession. Robust differentiation is a "fine motor skill" of teaching. Thus, few novice teachers will display great proficiency in planning and facilitating fully differentiated classrooms, and they should not be expected to do so. If they receive quality preservice preparation in differentiation, however, new teachers can begin their professional journeys with both the gross motor skills and some of the fine motor skills that are the foundation of responsive teaching. Teacher education programs and schools are wise to invest vigorously and consistently in continuing development of the skill and will of early teachers to succeed in academically diverse classrooms.

Teacher education programs and school districts that employ novice teachers should do the following:

• Set clear expectations for the novice's growth in student-centered, responsive instruction.

• Provide clear models of differentiated curriculum and differentiated instruction in action.

• Provide mentoring that helps teachers reflect on student needs and appropriate responses to those needs.

• Ensure teachers' comfort in implementing a growing range of instructional strategies that invite differentiation and facilitate its management.

• Provide early partnerships with teachers who practice differentiation.

• Provide the time and structure teachers need to reflect on and plan for student needs.

• Recognize growth toward responsive instruction in meaningful ways.

• • •

As schools become increasingly diverse, their capacity to provide a meaningful and empowering education for all individuals is directly related to our willingness to invest the time, resources, and guidance needed for beginning teachers to move away from teach-to-the-middle instruction. We must help all educators move toward teaching that meets individuals at their points of readiness, interest, and learning profile.

A Final Thought

Leading means going first, and in going first, you can trust me, for I have tested the ice. I have lived. I now know something of the rewards as well as the trappings of growing toward adulthood and making a world for yourself. Although the going first is no guarantee of success (because the world is not without risks and dangers), in the pedagogical relationship, there is a more fundamental guarantee: No matter what, I am here. And you can count on me.

Max van Manen, *The Tact of Teaching*

For many teachers, the classroom is the place where we spend our entire careers. For 25 or 30 years, we mark the days and seasons with entering and leaving the solitary yet crowded room in which we learn and practice our profession. The classroom is the place where we spend the better part of our lifetimes trying to make a difference.

It is a paradox of teaching that no two days are alike; yet, if we are not careful, all the days can take on a deadening sameness. We are wise to remember that we have every opportunity to transform ourselves and our practice, just as we have every opportunity to stagnate and remain much the same teachers we were when we began.

The ideas presented in this book are ambitious. They also are well within the reach of teachers who seek daily to do what we ought to ask of all students: risk, stretch, and push a bit beyond our comfort zone.

Lewis Thomas (1983) suggests that, as a human race, we should celebrate our ignorance rather than pretend we have many answers to life's complexities. "We can take some gratification at having come a certain distance," he says, "but it should be a deeper satisfaction, even an exhilaration, to realize we still have such a distance to go" (p. 163).

So it is with teaching, and that is the spirit of this book: neither to mourn what we have not done nor to rest on our victories but rather to look at all the reasons we have to show up again tomorrow at the classroom door, ready to join our students—every one of our students—in learning genuinely important things. The students who come to us will be vulnerable. They will come carrying nascent dreams. They will come dependent upon us to help them write a story of opportunity, effort, and success that will both commend the electricity of learning to the human mind and reinforce their capacity as learners. Every day, those of us who teach will decide whether to look beyond those realities and teach as though they did not exist or to embrace the terrifying and humanizing opportunity to be co-architects with our students of developing lives.

Rightly understood, excellent teaching is, in great measure, leadership of the young. I believe the assertion (Williamson, 1992) that our greatest fear as humans (and teachers) is not that we are inadequate in that role but that we are powerful beyond measure.

For me, differentiation is a manifestation of my acceptance of that power—and an unwillingness to look past the very particular needs that come into the classroom with every student every day. It is my commitment to respond to those needs—sometimes haltingly, often imperfectly—but always with the intent to say to the young person, "I see you. I care. I am here for you. You can count on me."

Appendix: Tools to Guide Planning for Differentiated Instruction

Tool 1: Elements, Attributes, and Instructional Strategies for Effective Differentiation

This tool presents a general model for thinking about how to differentiate instruction in diverse classrooms. First, it summarize, the characteristics of the quality **content, processes** (or sense-making activities), and **products** (summative assignments or other authentic assessments) that all learners should experience. These requirements should be at the center of all teacher planning, whether the teacher is thinking about how to present content, develop processes, or create assignments for the whole class or in response to specific student readiness levels, interests, or learning profiles.

Following each set of requirements are sample instructional strategies a teacher can use to differentiate content, processes, and products in response to readiness, interest, or learning profile. Although these lists are not exhaustive, they do reflect a current understanding of effective educational process. Note that all instructional strategies should be appropriate for both content requirements and student needs.

Effective Differentiation: Elements, Attributes, and Instructional Strategies		
Content Requirements	**Process Requirements**	**Product Requirements**
• Clear goals for knowledge, understanding, and skill (KUDs)	• Clear goals for knowledge, understanding, and skill, tightly aligned with content KUDs	• Clear goals for knowledge, understanding, and skill, tightly aligned with content KUDs
• Concept and understanding based	• Concept and understanding based	• Concept and understanding based
• High relevance	• Focused	• Skills of planning taught and required
• Engaging	• High level	• Skills of production taught and required
• Coherent	• Purposeful	• Requires integration and transfer of all key content KUDs
• Transferable	• Aims at transfer	
• Powerful	• Balances critical and creative thought	• Authentic problems, real audiences
• Authentic to the discipline	• Promotes metacognition	• Multiple modes of expression
• Multiple modes of teaching and student "intake"	• Multiple modes of expression	

Strategies for Differentiating Content	Strategies for Differentiating Process	Strategies for Differentiating Product
• Multiple texts and supplementary print resources • Varied internet resources • Varied audio and visual resources • Varied support mechanisms for reading • Modeling/demonstrations • Varied time allotments • Interest-based materials • Small-group instruction • Mini-workshops • Multiple teaching modes • Etc.	• Tiered assignments • Learning centers • Interest centers • Graphic organizers • Tri-mind options • Models of student work at different degrees of complexity • Varied modes of exploration and expression • Varied working arrangements • Learning contracts • Simulations • Complex instruction tasks • RAFT assignments • Literature or discussion circles • Web quests/web inquiry • Etc.	• Complex instruction products • Tri-mind options • Varied working arrangements • Varied resource options • Community-based products • Mentorships • Independent study • Orbital studies • Graduated rubrics • Varied modes of expression • Use of varied media • Tiered product assignments • Varied scaffolding • Web quests/web inquiry • Etc.

Tool 2: The Equalizer

This tool, designed to resemble the controls on audio equipment that a listener can slide to the left or right to adjust tone, volume, balance, and so on, is a useful model for thinking about and planning for **readiness differentiation.** The continuums of the Equalizer suggest "settings" that a teacher can adjust in an effort to find the most appropriate challenge level for individual learners.

To differentiate for variance in learners' readiness levels for a particular task, a teacher should always begin with the goal of ensuring solid, focused, significant curriculum and instruction—content, processes, and products that meet the requirements articulated in Tool 1. With that established, the teacher can then think about moving one or more of the Equalizer controls toward the left (more basic) or right (more complex) to adjust the initial task for a learner's starting point. For example, a learner who knows a great deal about the planets and who reads quite well might need to use relatively complex research resources to prepare for tomorrow's presentation. A classmate who doesn't read well and whose background knowledge on planets is less extensive may need more basic research materials to prepare for the presentation.

The Equalizer: A Tool for Planning Readiness-Based Differentiation

1. Information, Ideas, Materials, Applications

Foundational ———————————————— **Transformational**

2. Representations, Ideas, Applications, Materials

Concrete ———————————————— **Abstract**

3. Resources, Research, Issues, Problems, Skills, Goals

Simple ———————————————— **Complex**

4. Disciplinary Connections, Directions, Stages of Development

Single Facet ———————————————— **Multiple Facets**

5. Application, Insight, Transfer

Small Leap ———————————————— **Great Leap**

6. Solutions, Decisions, Approaches

More Structured ———————————————— **More Open**

7. In Process, in Research, in Products

Clearly Defined Problems ———————————————— **Fuzzy Problems**

8. Planning, Designing, Monitoring

More Structured ———————————————— **More Open**

9. Pace of Study, Pace of Thought

Slower ———————————————— **Quicker**

As with an audio equalizer, it is not necessary to move all the controls at the same time. It's also important to note that students who may need several Equalizer controls moved toward the left when they begin work on a topic or skill should, as a unit progresses, need activities and products that steadily reflect movement of the controls toward the right in order both to reflect their growth and to support further growth. This progression should be the case for all students in a class, regardless of their point of entry into a topic of study.

Please note that these continuums are not exhaustive; in fact, it's a good reflective exercise for teachers to think about what they do to make tasks appropriate for the varied learners in their own classroom and then create additional continuums to customize the Equalizer.

Tool 3: Equalizer Descriptors

This tool is designed to help teachers and curriculum developers consider **ways to modify curriculum and instruction along the various continuums in the Equalizer in response to learner readiness.** For example, if a learner is struggling with a particular idea or skill, a teacher may want to design a task for that child that is *foundational* (basic). The key to getting one student to make the necessary mental connections or complete an application activity may be to ask him to work with an idea or skill in a way that is familiar—perhaps largely like the examples covered in a textbook or discussed in class or resembling personal experience. However, a learner in the same classroom who is already comfortable with the idea or skill may be ready to apply it in a way that is *transformational*—meaning, removed from text and class examples or removed from personal experience.

Remember that the goal of readiness differentiation is to provide students with work that is meaning-rich or understanding-focused and set at a challenge level that requires them to stretch themselves. Simultaneously, teachers must plan the scaffolding, or supports, students need in order to meet the challenge and reach the new, higher level. Once that happens, it is time to slide the Equalizer controls to the right so that the challenge, once again, seems a bit out of reach—and so that, once again, with appropriate support or scaffolding, all students can succeed.

Thinking About the Equalizer

1. Information, Ideas, Materials, Applications

Foundational ▭▭▭▭▭▭▭▭▭ **Transformational**

- Close to text or experience
- Export idea and skill to similar or familiar setting
- Use key idea or skills alone
- Fundamental skills and knowledge emphasized
- Fewer permutations of skills and ideas

- Removed from text or experience
- Export idea or skill to unexpected or unfamiliar setting
- Use key idea or skill with unrelated idea or skill
- Use but move beyond fundamental skills and knowledge
- More permutations of skills and ideas

2. Representations, Ideas, Applications, Materials

Concrete ▭▭▭▭▭▭▭▭▭ **Abstract**

- Hold in hands or hands-on
- Tangible
- Literal
- Physical manipulation
- Event based
- Event to principle
- Demonstrated and explained

- Hold in mind or "minds on"
- Intangible
- Symbolic or metaphorical
- Mental manipulation
- Idea based
- Principle without event
- Not demonstrated or explained

3. Resources, Research, Issues, Problems, Skills, Goals

Simple ▭▭▭▭▭▭▭▭▭ **Complex**

- Use idea or skill being taught
- Work with no, one, or few abstractions
- Emphasizes appropriateness
- Requires relatively less originality
- More common vocabulary
- More accessible readability

- Combine idea or skill being taught with those previously taught
- Work with multiple abstractions
- Emphasizes elegance
- Requires relatively more originality
- More advanced vocabulary
- More advanced readability

4. Disciplinary Connections, Directions, Stages of Development

Single Facet ▭▭▭▭▭▭▭▭▭ **Multiple Facets**

- Fewer parts
- Fewer steps
- Fewer stages

- More parts
- More steps
- More stages

5. Application, Insight, Transfer

Small Leap ▭▭▭▭▭▭▭▭▭ **Great Leap**

- Few unknowns
- Relative comfort with most elements
- Less need to change familiar elements
- Requires less flexible thought
- Few gaps in required knowledge
- More evolutionary

- Many unknowns
- Relative unfamiliarity with many elements
- More need to change familiar elements
- Requires more flexible thought
- Significant gaps in required knowledge
- More revolutionary

Thinking About the Equalizer (*continued*)

6. Solutions, Decisions, Approaches

More Structured | **More Open**

- More directions or more precise directions
- More modeling
- Relatively less student choice

- Fewer directions
- Less modeling
- Relatively more student choice

7. In Process, in Research, in Products

Clearly Defined Problems | **Fuzzy Problems**

- Few unknowns
- More algorithmic
- Narrower range of acceptable responses or approaches
- Only relevant data provided
- Problem specified

- More unknowns
- More heuristic
- Wider range of acceptable responses or approaches
- Extraneous data provided
- Problem unspecified or ambiguous

8. Planning, Designing, Monitoring

More Structured | **More Open**

- More teacher or adult guidance and monitoring on
  - problem identification
  - goal setting
  - establishing time lines
  - following time lines
  - securing resources
  - use of resources
  - criteria for success
  - formulation of a product
  - evaluation
- More teacher scaffolding
- Learning the skills of independence

- Less teacher or adult guidance and monitoring on
  - problem identification
  - goal setting
  - establishing time lines
  - following time lines
  - securing resources
  - use of resources
  - criteria for success
  - formulation of a product
  - evaluation
- Less teacher scaffolding
- Demonstrating the skills of independence

9. Pace of Study, Pace of Thought

Slower | **Quicker**

- More time to work
- More practice
- More teaching and reteaching
- Process more systematically
- Probe breadth and depth

- Less time to work
- Less practice
- Less teaching and reteaching
- Process more rapidly
- Hit the high points

Once again, these descriptors are not definitive, and teachers are encouraged to expand those they find here and create new sets of descriptors for their own custom Equalizers by thinking about what they do to make tasks appropriate for the varied learners in their own classroom and adding descriptors that reflect their way of adapting task difficulty based on student readiness.

Bibliography

Allan, S. (1991, March). Ability-grouping research reviews: What do they say about grouping and the gifted? *Educational Leadership, 48*(6), 60–65.

Arnow, H. (1954). *The dollmaker*. New York: Avon.

Ayres, W. (2010). *To teach: The journey of a teacher*. New York: Columbia University Press.

Barell, J. (1995). *Teaching for thoughtfulness: Classroom strategies to enhance intellectual development.* White Plains, NY: Longman.

Bauer, J. (1996). *Sticks*. New York: Yearling.

Bauer, J. (1997). Sticks: Between the lines. *Book Links, 6*(6), 9–12.

Beecher, M., & Sweeny, S. (2008). Closing the achievement gap with curriculum enrichment and differentiation: One school's story. *Journal of Advanced Academics, 19,* 502–530.

Ben-Hur, M. (2006). *Concept-rich mathematics instruction: Building a strong foundation for reasoning and problem solving.* Alexandria, VA: ASCD.

Berliner, D. (1986). In pursuit of the expert pedagogue. *Educational Researcher, 15*(7), 5–13.

Berte, N. (1975). *Individualizing education by learning contracts.* San Francisco: Jossey-Bass.

Bess, J. (Ed.). (1997). *Teaching well and liking it: Motivating faculty to teach effectively.* Baltimore, MD: The Johns Hopkins University Press.

Bluestein, J. (Ed.). (1995). *Mentors, masters and Mrs. MacGregor: Stories of teachers making a difference.* Deerfield Beach, FL: Health Communications.

Bondy, E., & Ross, D. (2008, September). The teacher as warm demander. *Educational Leadership, 66*(1), 54–58.

Brandwein, P. (1981). *Memorandum: On renewing schooling and education.* New York: Harcourt Brace Jovanovich.

Brown, M. (1949). *The important book.* New York: Harper & Row.

Burris, C., & Garrity, D. (2008). *Detracking for excellence and equity.* Alexandria, VA: ASCD.

Caine, R., & Caine, G. (1994). *Making connections: Teaching and the human brain* (Rev. ed.). Menlo Park, CA: Addison-Wesley.

Caine, R., & Caine, G. (1997). *Education on the edge of possibility.* Alexandria, VA: ASCD.

Cohen, E. (1994). *Designing groupwork: Strategies for the heterogeneous classroom* (2nd ed.). New York: Teachers College Press.

Csikszentmihalyi, M., Rathunde, K., & Whalen, S. (1993). *Talented teenagers: The roots of success and failure.* New York: Cambridge University Press.

Daniels, H. (2002). *Literature circles: Voice and choice in book clubs and reading groups.* Portland, ME: Stenhouse.

Danielson, C. (2007). *Enhancing professional practice: A framework for teaching* (2nd ed.). Alexandria, VA: ASCD.

Duke, D. (2004). *The challenges of educational change.* Boston: Pearson.

Dweck, C. (2000). *Self-theories: Their role in motivation, personality, and development.* Philadelphia: Psychology Press.

Dweck, C. (2008). *Mindset: The new psychology of success.* New York: Ballantine.

Earl, L. (2003). *Assessment as learning: Using classroom assessment to maximize student learning.* Thousand Oaks, CA: Corwin.

Erickson, H. (2007). *Concept-based curriculum and instruction for the thinking classroom.* Thousand Oaks, CA: Corwin.

Evans, R. (1996). *The human side of school change.* San Francisco: Jossey-Bass.

Fleischman, P. (1996). *Dateline: Troy.* Cambridge, MA: Candlewick Press.

Fullan, M. (1993). *Change forces: Probing the depths of educational reform.* Bristol, PA: Falmer Press.

Fullan, M. (2001a). *Leading in a culture of change.* San Francisco: Jossey-Bass.

Fullan, M. (2001b). *The new meaning of educational change* (3rd ed.). New York: Teachers College Press.

Fullan, M. G., & Stiegelbauer, S. (1991). *The new meaning of educational change* (2nd ed.). New York: Teachers College Press.

Gamoran, A. (1992, October). Synthesis of research: Is ability grouping equitable? *Educational Leadership, 50*(2), 11–17.

Gamoran, A., Nystrand, M., Berends, M., & LePore, P. (1995). An organizational analysis of the effects of ability grouping. *American Educational Research Journal, 32,* 687–715.

Gardner, H. (1991). *The unschooled mind. How children think and how schools should teach.* New York: Basic Books.

Gardner, H. (1993). *Multiple intelligences: The theory in practice.* New York: Basic Books.

Gardner, H. (1997). Reflections on multiple intelligences: Myths and messages. *Phi Delta Kappan, 78,* 200–207.

Grigorenko, E., & Sternberg, R. (1997). Styles of thinking, abilities, and academic performance. *Exceptional Children, 63,* 295–312.

Hattie, J. (2009). *Visible learning: A synthesis of over 800 meta-analyses relating to achievement.* New York: Routledge.

Hattie, J. (2012). *Visible learning for teachers: Maximizing impact on learning.* New York: Routledge.

Howard, P. (1994). *The owner's manual for the brain.* Austin, TX: Leornian Press.

Jensen, E. (1998). *Teaching with the brain in mind.* Alexandria, VA: ASCD.

Kennedy, M. (2005). *Inside teaching: How classroom life undermines reform.* Cambridge, MA: Harvard University Press.

Knowles, M. (1986). *Using learning contracts.* San Francisco: Jossey-Bass.

Konigsburg, E. L. (1996). *The view from Saturday.* New York: Atheneum Books for Young Readers.

Kulik, J., & Kulik, C. (1991). Ability grouping and gifted students. In N. Colangelo & G. Davis (Eds.), *Handbook of gifted education* (pp. 178–196). Boston: Allyn & Bacon.

Lasley, T. J., & Matczynski, T. J. (1997). *Strategies for teaching in a diverse society: Instructional models.* Belmont, CA: Wadsworth.

Lowry, L. (1993). *The giver.* Boston: Houghton Mifflin.

Madea, B. (1994). *The multiage classroom: An inside look at one community of learners.* Cypress, CA: Creative Teaching Press.

Marsh, H., Tautwein, U., Lüdtke, O., Baumert, J., & Köller, O. (2007). The big-fish-little-pond effect: Persistent negative effects of selective high schools on self-concept after graduation. *American Educational Research Journal, 44,* 631–669.

McTighe, J., & Wiggins, G. (2013). *Essential questions: Opening doors to student understanding.* Alexandria, VA: ASCD.

National Research Council. (1999). *How people learn: Brain, mind, experience, and school.* Washington, DC: National Academies Press.

National Research Council. (2005). *How students learn: History, mathematics, and science in the classroom.* Washington, DC: National Academies Press.

National Research Council. (2012). *A framework for K–12 science education: Practices, crosscutting concepts, and core ideas.* Washington, DC: National Academies Press.

Oakes, J. (1985). *Keeping track: How schools structure inequality.* New Haven, CT: Yale Press.

O'Connor, K. (2011). *A repair kit for grading: 15 fixes for broken grades* (2nd ed.). Boston: Pearson.

Ohanian, S. (1988). On stir-and-serve recipes for teaching. In K. Ryan & J. M. Cooper (Eds.), *Kaleidoscope: Readings in education* (pp. 56–61). Boston: Allyn & Bacon.

Paterson, K. (1977). *Bridge to Terabithia.* New York: HarperCollins.

Paterson, K. (1991). *Lyddie.* New York: Dutton.

Phenix, P. (1986). *Realms of meaning: A philosophy of the curriculum for general education.* Ventura, CA: Ventura County Superintendent of Schools Office.

Rasmussen, F. (2006). *Differentiated instruction as a means for improving achievement as measured by the American College Testing (ACT)* (Unpublished doctoral dissertation). Loyola University of Chicago School of Education.

Reis, S., Burns, D., & Renzulli, J. (1992). *Curriculum compacting: The complete guide to modifying the curriculum for high ability students.* Mansfield Center, CT: Creative Learning Press.

Reis, S., McCoach, B., Little, C., Muller, L., & Kaniskan, R. (2011). The effects of differentiated instruction and enrichment pedagogy on reading achievement in five elementary schools. *American Educational Research Journal, 48,* 462–501.

Robb, L. (1997). Talking with Paul Fleischman. *Book Links, 6*(4), 39–43.

Saint-Exupéry, A. (1943). *The little prince.* New York: Harcourt, Brace & World.

Santangelo, T., & Tomlinson, C. (2009). The application of differentiated instruction in postsecondary environments: Benefits, challenges, and future directions. *International Journal of Teaching and Learning in Higher Education, 20,* 307–323.

Sarason, S. (1990). *The predictable failure of educational reform: Can we change course before it's too late?* San Francisco: Jossey-Bass.

Sarason, S. (1993). *The case for change: Rethinking the preparation of educators.* San Francisco: Jossey-Bass.

Schiever, S. (1991). *A comprehensive approach to teaching thinking.* Boston: Allyn & Bacon.

Seaton, M., Marsh, H., & Craven, R. (2010). Big-fish-little-pond effect: Generalizability and moderation—Two sides of the same coin. *American Educational Research Journal, 47,* 390–433.

Sergiovanni, T. (1999). *Rethinking leadership.* Glenview, IL: Lab Light.

Sergiovanni, T. (2005). *Strengthening the heartbeat: Leading and learning together in schools.* San Francisco: Jossey-Bass.

Siegel, J., & Shaughnessy, M. (1994). Educating for understanding: A conversation with Howard Gardner. *Phi Delta Kappan, 75,* 564.

Sizer, T. (1992). *Horace's school: Redesigning the American high school.* Boston: Houghton Mifflin.

Slavin, R. (1987). Ability grouping and achievement in the elementary school: A best evidence synthesis. *Review of Educational Research, 57,* 293–336.

Slavin, R. (1993). Ability grouping in the middle grades: Achievement effects and alternatives. *Elementary School Journal, 93,* 535–552.

Sousa, D. (2010). How science met pedagogy. In D. Sousa (Ed.), *Mind, brain, and education: Neuroscience implications for the classroom* (pp. 8–24). Bloomington, IN: Solution Tree.

Sousa, D. (2011). *How the brain learns* (4th ed.). Thousand Oaks, CA: Corwin.

Sousa, D., & Tomlinson, C. (2011). *Differentiation and the brain: How neuroscience supports the learner-friendly classroom.* Bloomington, IN: Solution Tree.

Sternberg, R. (1985). *Beyond IQ: A triarchic theory of human intelligence.* New York: Cambridge University Press.

Sternberg, R. (1988). *The triarchic mind: A new theory of human intelligence.* New York: Viking.

Sternberg, R. (1997, March). What does it mean to be smart? *Educational Leadership, 54*(6), 20–24.

Sternberg, R., Torff, B., & Grigorenko, E. (1998). Teaching triarchically improves student achievement. *Journal of Educational Psychology, 90,* 374–384.

Stevenson, C. (1992). *Teaching ten to fourteen year olds* (3rd ed.). New York: Longman.

Stevenson, C. (1997). An invitation to join Team 21! In C. Tomlinson (Ed.), *In search of common ground: What constitutes appropriate curriculum and instruction for gifted middle schoolers?* (pp. 31–62). Washington, DC: National Association for Gifted Children.

Strachota, B. (1996). *On their side: Helping children take charge of their learning.* Greenfield, MA: Northeast Foundation for Children.

Stronge, J. (2002). *Qualities of effective teachers.* Alexandria, VA: ASCD.

Sylwester, R. (1995). *A celebration of neurons: An educator's guide to the human brain.* Alexandria, VA: ASCD.

Thomas, L. (1983). *Late night thoughts on listening to Mahler's ninth symphony.* New York: Bantam Books.

Tieso, C. (2002). *The effects of grouping and curricular practices on intermediate students' math achievement.* Hartford: National Research Center on the Gifted and Talented, University of Connecticut.

Tomlinson, C. (2003). *Fulfilling the promise of the differentiated classroom.* Alexandria, VA: ASCD.

Tomlinson, C. (2004). *How to differentiate instruction in mixed-ability classrooms* (2nd ed.). Alexandria, VA: ASCD.

Tomlinson, C., Brimijoin, K., & Narvaez, L. (2008). *The differentiated school: Making revolutionary changes in teaching and learning.* Alexandria, VA: ASCD.

Tomlinson, C., Callahan, C., Moon, T., Tomchin, E., Landrum, M., Imbeau, M., . . . Eiss, N. (1995). *Preservice teacher preparation in meeting the needs of gifted and other academically diverse students.* Charlottesville: National Research Center on the Gifted and Talented, University of Virginia.

Tomlinson, C., Callahan, C., Tomchin, C., Eiss, N., Imbeau, M., & Landrum, M. (1997). Becoming architects of communities of learning: Addressing academic diversity in contemporary classrooms. *Exceptional Children, 63,* 269–282.

Tomlinson, C., & Imbeau, M. (2010). *Leading and managing a differentiated classroom.* Alexandria, VA: ASCD.

Tomlinson, C., & McTighe, J. (2006). *Integrating differentiated instruction and understanding by design: Connecting content and kids.* Alexandria, VA: ASCD.

Tomlinson, C., & Moon, T. (2013). *Assessment in a differentiated classroom: A guide for student success.* Alexandria, VA: ASCD.

van Manen, M. (1991). *The tact of teaching: Toward a pedagogy of thoughtfulness.* Albany: State University of New York.

van Manen, M. (2003). *The tone of teaching.* New York: Scholastic.

Vygotsky, L. (1978). *Mind in society: The development of higher psychological processes* (M. Cole, V. John-Steiner, S. Scribner, & E. Souberman, Eds.). Cambridge, MA: Harvard University Press.

Vygotsky, L. (1986). *Thought and language* (A. Kozulin, Ed. & Trans.). Cambridge, MA: The MIT Press. (Original work published 1934.)

Watanabe, M. (2012). *"Heterogenius" classrooms: Detracking math and science.* New York: Teachers College Press.

Wiggins, G., & McTighe, J. (2005). *Understanding by design* (2nd ed.). Alexandria, VA: ASCD.

Williamson, M. (1992). *A return to love.* New York: HarperCollins

Willis, J. (2006). *Research-based strategies to ignite student learning.* Alexandria, VA: ASCD.

Willis, J. (2010). The current impact of neuroscience on teaching and learning. In D. Sousa (Ed.), *Mind, brain, and education: Neuroscience implications for the classroom* (pp. 44–66). Bloomington, IN: Solution Tree.

Wolfe, P. (2010). *Brain matters: Translating research into classroom practice* (2nd ed.). Alexandria, VA: ASCD.

Index

About the Author

Carol Ann Tomlinson is William Clay Parrish, Jr. Professor and Chair of Educational Leadership, Foundations, and Policy and co-director of the Institutes on Academic Diversity at the Curry School of Education, University of Virginia. She works throughout the United States and internationally with educators who want to create classrooms that are more responsive to a broad range of learners.

Carol's experience as an educator includes 21 years as a public school teacher working with preschoolers, middle school students, and high school students. At the secondary level, she taught English, language arts, German, and history. She also administered district-level programs for struggling and advanced learners and was Virginia's Teacher of the Year in 1974.

At the University of Virginia, Carol teaches undergraduates, master's students, and doctoral students, predominantly in the areas of curriculum design and differentiated instruction. She was named Outstanding Professor at Curry School of Education in 2004 and received an All-University Teaching Award in 2008. She has written more than 300 books, book chapters, articles, and other materials for educators, and her books have been translated into 12 languages. In 2014's *EducationNext* Edu-Scholar Public Presence rankings, she was named one of the two most influential higher education voices in the United States in Psychology and the 16th most influential in all education-related fields.

Related ASCD Resources: Differentiated Instruction

At the time of publication, the following ASCD resources were available (ASCD stock numbers appear in parentheses). For up-to-date information about ASCD resources, go to www.ascd.org. You can search the complete archives of *Educational Leadership* at http://www.ascd.org/el.

ASCD EDge Group

Exchange ideas and connect with other educators interested in differentiated instruction, multiple intelligences, and the While Child on the social networking site ASCD EDge™ at http://ascdedge.ascd.org/

Online Courses

Differentiated Instruction: An Introduction (#PD11OC115M)
Differentiated Instruction: Creating an Environment That Supports Learning (#PD11OC118)
Differentiated Instruction: Teaching with Student Differences in Mind (#PD11OC138)

Print Products

Assessment and Student Success in a Differentiated Classroom by Carol Ann Tomlinson and Tonya R. Moon (#108028)

Differentiation in Practice: A Resource Guide for Differentiating Curriculum, Grades K–5 by Carol Ann Tomlinson and Caroline Cunningham Eidson (#102294)

Differentiation in Practice: A Resource Guide for Differentiating Curriculum, Grades 5–9 by Carol Ann Tomlinson and Caroline Cunningham Eidson (#102293)

Differentiation in Practice: A Resource Guide for Differentiating Curriculum, Grades 9–12 by Carol Ann Tomlinson and Cindy A. Strickland (#104140)

Fulfilling the Promise of the Differentiated Classroom: Strategies and Tools for Responsive Teaching by Carol Ann Tomlinson (#103107)

Integrating Differentiated Instruction & Understanding by Design: Connecting Content and Kids by Carol Ann Tomlinson and Jay McTighe (#105004)

Leading and Managing a Differentiated Classroom by Carol Ann Tomlinson and Marcia B. Imbeau (#108011)

Task Rotation: Strategies for Differentiating Activities and Assessments by Learning Style (A Strategic Teacher PLC Guide) by Harvey F. Silver, Joyce W. Jackson, and Daniel R. Moirao (#110129)

Video

At Work in the Differentiated Classroom (DVD) (#601071)
Differentiated Instruction in Action (3-DVD series) (#608050)

THE WHOLE CHILD The Whole Child Initiative helps schools and communities create learning environments that allow students to be healthy, safe, engaged, supported, and challenged. To learn more about other books and resources that relate to the whole child, visit www.wholechildeducation.org.

For more information: send e-mail to member@ascd.org; call 1-800-933-2723 or 703-578-9600, press 2; send a fax to 703-575-5400; or write to Information Services, ASCD, 1703 N. Beauregard St., Alexandria, VA 22311-1714 USA.